VEGETARIAN CATERING

COMMODITIES, TECHNIQUES & PROCESSES

Richard Davies MHCIMA
Senior Lecturer, Plymouth College of Further Education

Contributions by:

Joan Bristow B.Sc. (Hons).
Lecturer, Plymouth College of Further Education

Peter Odgers FHCIMA., Cert.Ed.
Senior Lecturer, Westminster College

Gale Odgers Publications Ltd.,
High Cross House, Millbrook, Cornwall PL10 1DX

© Gale Odgers Publications Ltd.
   First Published 1987

This book is copyright and may not be reproduced in whole or in part (except for review purposes) without express permission of the publishers in writing.

British Library Cataloguing in Publication Data.

Davies, Richard 1946 —
   Vegetarian Catering.
   1. Vegetarian Cookery
   I. Title
   641.5'6346   TX837

ISBN 0-94831-510-5

Typeset in England by PICA, Biggin Hill, Kent.
Printed by: PDS Printers, Cattedown, Plymouth.
Cover Design by: Planographic, Plymouth.
Photographs by: Peter Belton & Anna Horwood.

Hotel, Catering and Leisure Operations

A Study Series

GALE ODGERS PUBLICATIONS Ltd.

GENERAL EDITOR: K.J. Gale B.A.(Hons)., Cert.Ed.
TECHNICAL EDITOR: P.F. Odgers FHCIMA., Cert.Ed.

This book is dedicated to my wife Wendy and children, Matthew and Nicola for their help and patience during it's writing.

Vegetarian Catering — Contents

Chapter 1: **The Development of Vegetarian Catering** 1

Chapter 2: **Vegetarian Commodities** 9
    Beans & Pulses 10
    Dairy Products 14
    Dried Fruits 19
    Edible Fungi 21
    Grains & Flours 24
    Herbs 30
    Nuts & Seeds 36
    Sea Vegetables 40
    Soya Products 43
    Spices 45

Chapter 3: **Basic Preparation** 53
    Grains & Pulses 54
    Pastries 57
    Stocks & Sauces 62
    Dressings 70
    Batters 76
    Information 78

Chapter 4: **Techniques & Catering Applications** 80
    Cooking Methods 81
    Preparation & Techniques 88
    Menu Planning 92
    Nutrition 101
    Commodity Purchase Sizes 109

Chapter 5: **Processes & Recipes — Starting Courses** 113
    Cocktails & Patés 114
    Dips, Mousses & Vegetable Dishes 117
    Soups 120
    Egg & Soufflé Dishes 130

Chapter 6:	**Processes & Recipes — Main Courses**	140
	Vegetables & Potatoes	140
	Grains	150
	Pulses	168
	Nuts & Seeds	173
	Salads	176
Chapter 7:	**Processesd & Recipes — Sweets & Savouries**	182
	Hot Sweets	183
	Cold Sweets	188
	Snacks	198
Appendix 1:	**Further Reading**	203
Appendix 2:	**User Activities**	204
Index:	....	206

LIST OF PHOTOGRAPHS

1.	Poached Egg with Cheese & Spinach	129
2.	Miso Soup	132
3.	Hot Suffed Mushrooms	133
4.	Stir-fried Vegetables in a basket	153
5.	Vegetarian Suet Pudding	157
6.	Savoury Fillo Cake	160
7.	Bean Bag	177
8.	Vegetable Salad	181
9.	Raspberry & Peach Wendy	195
10.	Egg Roll	199

Acknowledgements

David Ashen, Head of the Hotel and Catering Department, Plymouth College of Further Education, Harry Cunningham, Tony Curnow, Dave Hopkins, Eric Lile, Margaret Smith, Dave Jonas, Roland Haddy, Sue Williams, Barbara Wenmoth and others from the college for their help and support.
The Milk Marketing Board for the use of their technical information on milk and milk products.
Barbican Wholefoods, Plymouth for supplying samples of commodities.
Devon Herbs (Proprietors H.F. & S.A. Wetherbee) for supplying samples of fresh herbs.
Wagstaff China and the Chez Nous Restaurant, Plymouth for supplying china and glass.
Micro Audit Ltd for supplying tempeh starter.
David Davies, my father, for his help with indexing.
Bill Scott for his help with information on dried fruit.
The first group of B/TEC Vegetarian students at Plymouth College of Further Education for their help in testing the recipes.
The Vegetarian Society UK Ltd, for their help and support and for supplying valuable background information.
John Lanning for producing the line drawings.
Gwyneth Pearce and Rebecca Beale for their help to Joan Bristow in compiling the Nutrition Section.
Alan Wills for computer graphics.
The Realeat Company

Preface

This book has been written for all those who are interested in vegetarian food, in particular students and caterers who require a good basic knowledge of those commodities and processes involved in the production of vegetarian dishes.

Not only is the book designed to provide a comprehensive introduction to many aspects of vegetarian food preparation but also it covers the food production requirements for the new B/TEC Ordinary National Diploma in Hotel Catering and Institutional Operations (Vegetarian) and the City and Guilds 719 Vegetarian Cookery Certificate.

The chapter explaining the development of Vegetarianism and Vegetarian catering together with the introductions to the other chapters have been written by Peter Odgers.

The book provides information on the various vegetarian food products and methods of cooking along with a comprehensive set of nutritional information written by Joan Bristow.

The Basic Preparations have been written and provided to give foundation recipes for the processes of food production that follow. The process of production of dishes has been given priority over the ingredients, this is to encourage the reader to adapt the recipes using ingredients that are readily available and in season, thus creating many variations of a particular dish.

Useful additional information and student questions and exercises have been provided to help those wishing to set up a product testing situation. Finally, the book has been written not so much as a rigid set of rules but as a guide to the commodities, preparations and processes involved in the production of vegetarian dishes.

Richard M. Davies

The Development of Vegetarian Catering

'Food is essential to all but considered by few'. This is a statement which could be applied to the Seventies and the general public's attitude towards what was eaten. We have seen, however, in recent years, a far greater awareness by the same general public of the food it eats, particularly with regard to health. Concern expressed by experts in food and health regarding what we eat and how it may be related to various diseases, has received increasing amounts of publicity through the mass media. This has happened to such an extent that food producers and retailers now go to great pains to explain to their customers that their products are 'additive free', 'low fat' content and have 'only natural products used'. Animal meat and fat have been proven to be a principal cause of heart disease. A consequence of this fact has been for people to minimise or eliminate their consumption of those related products. We also must consider that, as a matter of conscience, an increasing number of people think it wrong to consume the meat of a creature that once lived and breathed. To a greater extent some think it wrong to consume any product derived from a living creature. There are many schools of thought in this area, Richard Davies has defined the different types of vegetarian at the end of this introduction.

It would be wrong, however, to think that vegetarianism is some new development or a passing fad. Vegetarianism can be traced back to the early Christians and early writers known to have endorsed or be committed to vegetarianism include Plato, Socrates, Pythagoras and Ovid. There is proof that a vegetarian movement existed throughout the ages but not in an organised form until the nineteenth century. The Vegetarian Society was formed in 1847 with its first annual general meeting in Haywards Hotel, Manchester with 232 of its 478 members attending a dinner afterwards. This is one of the first recorded vegetarian catering functions. Whilst the Society was Manchester based and still is today, London followed suit in 1849 with its own branch and during the 1850s many branches were started throughout the country. Prominent in the Society at this time was a Mr Joseph Brotherton MP who's wife had published the first vegetarian cookery book. Other supporters were George Bernard Shaw, Count Tolstoi and Mr and Mrs Bramwell Booth of the Salvation Army. Since its outset the Vegetarian Society has published its own magazine. The first magazine 'Vegetarian Messenger' had a circulation of over 4,000 copies and since then a number of magazines have appeared under various titles. The current magazine, 'The Vegetarian', is a bi-monthly publication with a circulation of over 50,000. The current membership of the Vegetarian Society is over 20,000 and has offices in Manchester and London. The Society has an active youth section, organises cookery courses in different parts of the country and one of its main aims is to provide for the educational needs of vegetarianism. It has done this by establishing a research scholarship at Reading University; other research is carried out by the Vegetarian Nutritional Research Centre at Watford. There are several other organisations linked to the vegetarian movement, including the Vegan Society and the Vegetarian Children's Charity which provides homes for needy vegetarian children; other societies run homes for the elderly.

A prominent researcher of vegetarianism, Maxwell Lee wrote in the 1970s: 'We can look forward to a most exciting period in the development of the vegetarian movement'. The truth of this statement has been born out by the results of various surveys undertaken by the food industry. The Realeat Company have commissioned Gallup Poll each year since

NON MEATEATERS
THREE YEARS OF CHANGE

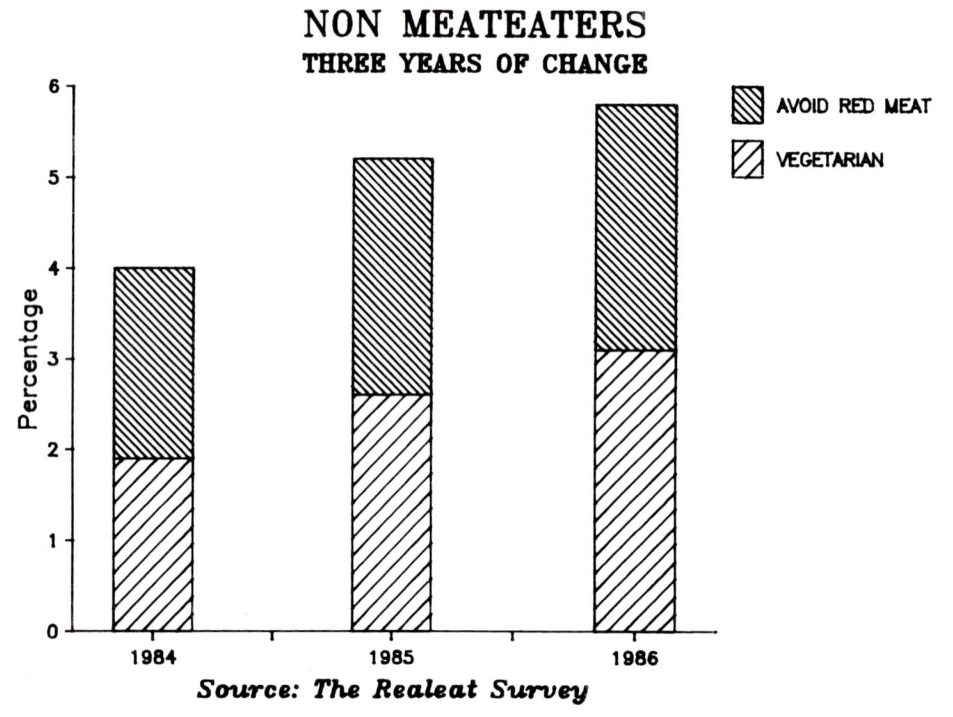

Source: The Realeat Survey

Table 1: Non-meat eaters percentage of population 1984-86

1984 to conduct a market research survey into Britain's changing attitudes to meat eating. They carry out an investigation of the general public by asking if they were vegetarian or if they avoided red meat. They produced results as to their sex, age group, location, socio-economic group and the reasons why they did not eat meat.

Table one shows an increase of 30% between 1984 and 1985 and a further increase of 11% between 1985 and 1986, therefore during the three years of the survey it shows an overall increase of 45%. This 1986 survey shows that approximately 1.5 million of the population are vegetarian and 1.7 million avoid red meat.

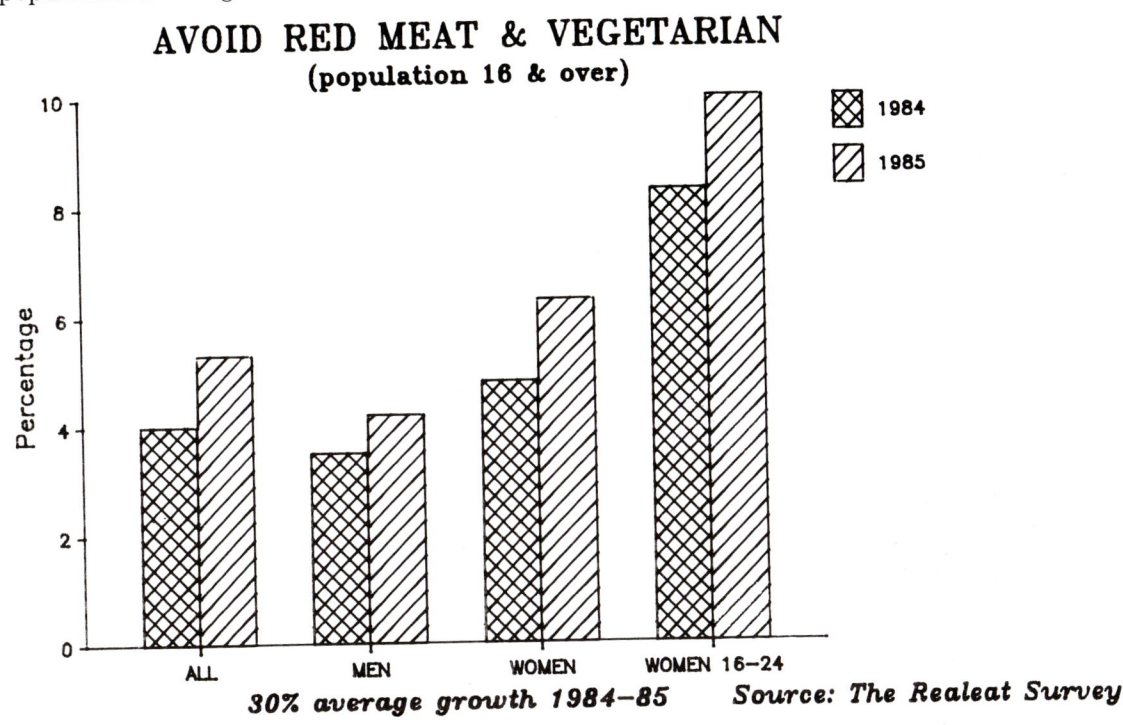

AVOID RED MEAT & VEGETARIAN
(population 16 & over)

30% average growth 1984–85   Source: The Realeat Survey

Table 2: Vegetarian and non-red meat eaters by sex, and female age group 16-24 1984-85

Table two shows a breakdown, firstly by sex, in which there are at least 50% more women than men who avoid red meat or who are vegetarian. In addition, of the age groups surveyed, 9.9% of the female population between 16 and 24 have these preferences. The table shows an average 30% growth over the period surveyed. It must be remembered that these are surveys of the total, male, female and 16-24 groups of the population and that the percentages are expressed of the respective group.

EATING LESS MEAT FOR REASONS OF HEALTH
BY REGION, 1986 COMPARED TO 1985

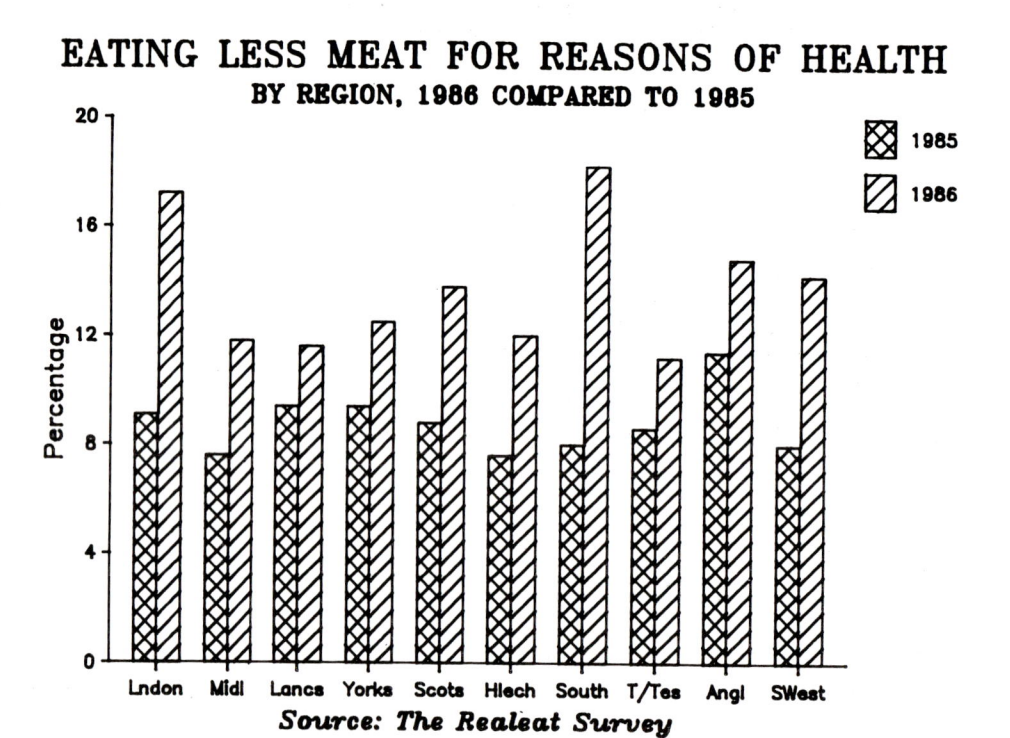

Source: The Realeat Survey

Table 3: Eating less meat for reasons of health by region 1985-86.

Table three shows the percentage of the population in each of the regions who eat less meat for health reasons. A further breakdown of this survey showed that 35% eat less meat for all reasons and an average of 14.2% for health reasons. It is noticeable that there is a higher proportion of the population in the southern half of Great Britain who eat less meat.

Table four shows the reasons for eating less meat, either through choice (health, moral or taste) or because of cost. A further breakdown showed that an average of 16.5% of the population eat less meat through choice as against 12% through cost. Scotland showed a reversal of this trend with 18.4% due to cost and 3.2% giving a variety of other reasons. We would expect income groups A B & C to eat less meat through choice, whereas groups D & E are more likely to do so for reasons of cost.

REASONS FOR EATING LESS MEAT
INCOME GROUP

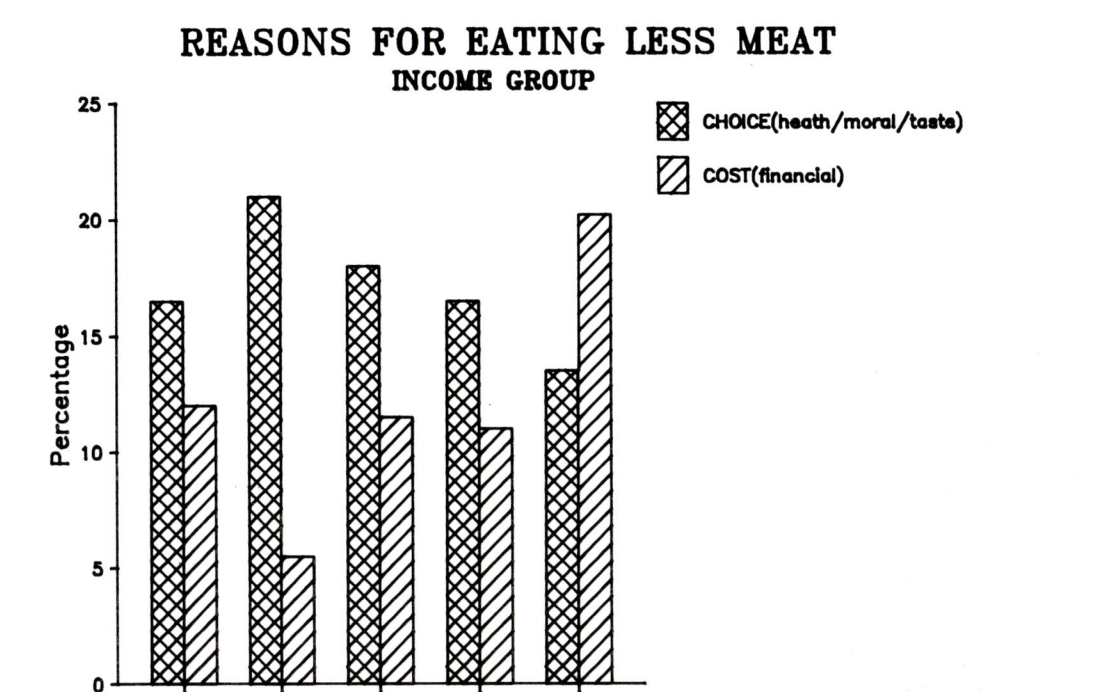

Table 4: Reasons for eating less meat by income group 1984-85

Other surveys have revealed that between 1980 and 1985 fresh fish sales have increased by 40%, 59% of housewives buy wholemeal bread regularly, 60% of housewives actively try to avoid buying fatty foods and 90% use salads to create a healthy and balanced diet. The growth in health food shops between 1975 and 1985 has been over

What the public eats in their own homes the catering industry must follow and we are able to see the industry's response. One of the pioneers of vegetarian catering who ran vegetarian restaurants in Germany before opening the Vega Restaurant in London in 1934 was Walter Fliess. He was instrumental in setting up the first vegetarian class at Hotelympia in 1954, in the first year he was requested to become the maitre concern. Together with his wife he wrote 'Classic Vegetarian Cookery' published by Penguin which may well be regarded as the first vegetarian catering text book.

100%, latest figures show there are now approaching 2,000 throughout the country. This does not include the introduction of health food departments into all the major supermarkets.

We have already mentioned homes for young and elderly vegetarians in the late nineteenth and early twentieth centuries. It is not until the late 1970s that we have seen a response of any scale from the industry, indeed in some sectors and in many individual operations it is only now happening. The development of specialist operations was centred around London and other major cities at the outset, with the first restaurants opening in the 1920s. These establishments were, in general, Indian or Oriental almost to the exclusion of others. It was not until the 1960s that restaurants specialising in wholefoods and vegetarian foods spread outside the main centres of population. 'Cranks' the most well known vegetarian restaurant group opened their first restaurant in London in 1961, they now have 5 establishments in operation, with plans to further expand in 1987 by possibly offering franchises on their theme and name.

As demand has grown during the last twenty years, so the number of establishments has increased. During this period we have also seen the inclusion of non-meat dishes on the menus of many different operations, both commercial and industrial/institutional. The 1980s has seen the most rapid growth in both specialist operations and the awareness in all sectors of the industry of the need to supply the increasing demand for non-meat eaters. Instead of offering omelettes, quiches or salads, as they have done in the past, caterers have had to re-think their menus to offer a greater variety of dishes for this market. Demand has increased rapidly from industrial canteens, school meals and institutional establishments, to such an extent that existing staff have had to be retrained. Specialist operations tend to be run by vegetarians for vegetarians and consequently they have a more varied and imaginative approach, probably through their own interest or by attending courses run by the Vegetarian Association. To meet the needs of the industry, courses have been set up by the Business and Technical Education Council and City and Guilds. The first of these courses started at Plymouth College of Further Education in 1985 in response to Beverley Chip canvassing every catering college in the country to run such a course. David Ashen, the Head of the Catering Department at Plymouth realised the potential demand for such a course and appointed Richard Davies to research and set up a BTEC Diploma Course. Other colleges in regional centres are planning to start similar courses in the next few years.

This book is the first vegetarian catering text book, to be published to meet the demand from the hotel and catering industry for knowlege of the wide range of commodities available and the application of traditional basic preparations, techniques and processes used in the industry and how they may be applied to vegetarian dishes and menus. As the general public becomes increasingly aware of healthy eating, so the demand for specialist establishments, menus and dishes will continue to grow. Many of the good food guides have vegetarian classifications and there are several regional and national guide books which specialise in vegetarian establishments. It is predicted that by the end of the 1980s there will be some 1,500 specialist establishments catering for vegetarians and that 99% of all catering establishments will offer a selection of non-meat dishes for their customers to choose from.

This book has been written to satisfy the need for a text book about Vegetarian Catering. It explains the different commodities that may be used and how accepted techniques, skills and processes used in the food preparation industry may be adapted for vegetarian establishments.

Peter Odgers
Senior Lecturer
Westminster College

Definition of Vegetarianism

There are two main vegetarian diets, 'Vegan' and 'Lacto-vegetarian'.

Vegan
This is the more restricted of the two diets, forbidding the consumption and use of all products from a living or dead creature, animal, fish, bird or insect.

In practical catering terms this means a diet excluding all animal milk products, eggs, meat, fish and in some cases honey.

A person following a vegan diet will also refrain from wearing shoes and clothes made from animal products, wool, leather etc.

Lacto-Vegetarian
The vast majority of vegetarians follow this diet, which forbids the consumption of flesh, animal, fish, bird or insect. However, foods which are obtained without harm from a living animal such as eggs and milk may be consumed.

Although most milk products are acceptable, cheese obtained from normal suppliers is not, due to the use of rennin, an enzyme obtained from the stomach of a calf, which is used to curdle the milk in making the cheese.

Cheese made from non-animal rennin can be obtained from specialist suppliers.

Other Related Diets
Fruit Diet
This is a strict vegetarian diet requiring that only the fruits of plants may be eaten; in other words nuts, fruits, pulses and seeds are permissible but not leaves, roots or stems, eg. spinach, carrots or celery.

Macrobiotic
This is not a true vegetarian diet but more a way of life and healthy eating. The word Macrobiotic means 'Large life'. George Ohsawa derived the philosophy from the ancient cultures of India, China and Japan. Today the philosophy has a very strong following in the USA.

The diet divides foods into 'Yin' and 'Yang', leaves or foods from above the ground and roots and foods from below the ground. Fish, meat and poultry can be eaten but only in small amounts and are essentially Yang foods, whereas dairy foods are essentially Yin.

To the caterer this diet requires a good balance of root and leaf vegetables with small amounts of fish, meat, poultry and dairy produce.

CHAPTER 2
Vegetarian Commodities

It is important that all caterers have an extensive knowledge of the commodities that are available to them and, for practical purposes, their availability. The caterer should be able to compare the various types of fresh and convenience commodity, with regard to their quality, price, storage and the preparation costs involved. In this chapter the author has put the commodities available for vegetarian catering in to the groups listed below for easy reference purposes.

Beans & Pulses	Herbs
Dairy Products	Nuts & Seeds
Dried Fruits	Sea Vegetables
Edible Fungi	Soya Products
Grains & Flours	Spices

Whilst these groups can be directly applied to vegetarian catering and the techniques and processes used later in the book, the list is by no means exhaustive. The author has deliberately omitted commodities for which information is widely available in many catering text books and similar publications. For example, vegetables which in general form the basis of almost all vegetarian meals have been omitted because it is regarded that caterers will already have knowledge of them.

Two important considerations when selecting commodities are what market the end product is aimed at and how much the customers are prepared to pay for them. These considerations will help the caterer to decide whether or not to use convenience or fresh foods and foods in or out of season as the case may be. The caterer must also decide the most economic method of purchasing commodities. He should take into consideration the commodities' prices, its shelf life to maintain quality and the storage facilities available to him. At the end of this chapter is a guide to commodity purchase sizes which will assist the caterer when deciding the most economic ordering quantity for any particular ingredient.

Commodities — Beans & Pulses

Beans & Pulses

Aduki Beans
Other Names: Adzuki Beans (Phaseolus angularis).
Description: Small 0.5cm long red in colour.
Area of Production: Far East — China and Japan.
Availability: All year.

Black-eye Beans
Other Names: (Vigna unguiculata) Cowpeas, Black-eyed Peas.
Description: Medium sized, approximately 1cm in length, creamy white in colour with a black 'eye' spot.
Area of Production: Central Africa and America.
Availability: All year.

Broad Beans
Other Names: (Vicia faba) Fara, Faba, Ful Medames.
Description: Large, 1.5-2cm in size, pale green in colour when fresh, pale brown when dried.
Area of Production: Europe.
Availability: Fresh late summer.

Butter Beans
Other Names: (Phaseolus lunatus) Fava Beans.
Description: Large 1.5-2cm in size, white in colour and kidney shaped.
Area of Production: South and Middle America.
Availability: All year.

Commodities — Beans & Pulses

Canellini
Other Names: (Phaseolus vulgaris).
Description: Medium size, 1cm in length, white and kidney shaped, a variety of the Kidney Bean.
Area of Production: Italy and South America.
Availability: All year.

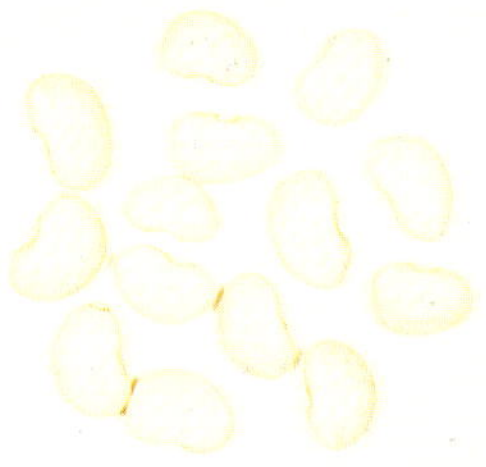

Chinese Black Bean
Other Names: (Glycine mac)
Description: Small 0.25cm in length, Black Soya Bean, sold as fermented paste in Chinese shops.
Area of Production: China, Far East.
Availability: All year.

Chick Peas
Other Names: (Cicer avietinum) Bengal gram, Garbanzo beans.
Description: Medium size, 0.5-1cm in diameter and creamy white in colour.
Area of Production: Turkey and Mediterranean countries and India.
Availability: All year.

Field Beans
Other Names: (Vieia faba) British Horse Bean, Tic & Daffa Bean.
Description: Medium size, 0.5cm round to oval, oak brown in colour.
Area of Production: Native of the British Isles.
Availability: All year.

Commodities — Beans & Pulses

Flageolet Beans
Other Names: (Phaseolus vulgaris).
Description: Medium size, 1cm in length, kidney shaped, pale green in colour.
Area of Production: Europe.
Availability: All year.

Haricot Beans
Other Names: (Phaseolus vulgaris) Pea Beans, Navy Beans.
Description: Medium size, 0.5cm in length, creamy white in colour.
Area of Production: North America.
Availability: All year.

Kidney Beans — Red, Black, Pinto or Speckled, Cranberry, Great Northern Bean, Coco Bean
Other Names: Black Beans, Zebra Beans (Phaseolus vulgaris).
Description: Medium sized, 1cm in length with black, red or speckled brown colour, white red speckled or large smooth white.
Area of Production: America.
Availability: All year.

Lima Beans
Other Names: (Phaseolus vulgaris)
Description: Medium sized, 1cm in length, similar to, but smaller than, Butter Beans.
Area of Production: America.
Availability: All year.

Commodities — Beans & Pulses

Mung Beans
Other Names: (Phaseolus aureus).
Description: Small 0.5cm in length, bright green kidney shaped, can also be split and dried.
Area of Production: Asia.
Availability: All year.

Soya Bean
Other Names: Glycine Max.
Description: A small, round pale yellow bean.
Area of Production: China and USA.
Availability: All year round.

Lentils — Red, Brown, Green, Continental
Other Names: (lens esculenta)
Description: Brown — small, 0.25cm in length round reddish brown: Red-brown lentils with the husk removed also split: Green and Continental, medium sized, 0.5cm in length, flat round and pale green in colour.
Area of Production: Red and brown Northern Europe and Mediterranean Countries: Green and Continental: Russia, America and Mediterranean Countries.
Availability: All year.

Peas — Whole green, split yellow and green
Other Names: (Pisum sativum).
Description: Approximately 0.5-1cm in diameter, when whole, pale green to white or darker green, in colour. When split also orange/yellow.
Area of Production: Europe
Availability: All year.

13

Commodities — Dairy Products

Dairy Products

Pasteurised milk
Description:

Mild heat treated to 72°C for 15 seconds, followed by rapid cooling to below 10°C. 3.8% fat. 380 Calories per pint.

Availability:

All year, sold in bottles with silver tops or disposable containers.

Homogenised milk
Description:

Milk is Homogenised by forcing it through a fine aperture to break it down into fat globules. These do not rise to the surface but remain in suspension. The milk is then pasteurised. 3.8% fat. 380 Calories per pint.

Availability:

All year, sold in bottles with a red top or carton packs, Milkpak 3-5 gals, Chumpak or Handipak 5 gals, Portabag 3 gals, Churnbox 3-5 gals, Carrypak 3-5 gals.

Channel Island milk
Description:

The milk is pasteurised from Jersey or Guernsey breeds 4.8% fat. 445 calories per pint.

Availability:

All year, sold in bottles with Gold Tops.

Semi Skimmed milk
Description:

This milk contains half the fat content of whole milk and is homogenised and pasteurised. 1.5-1.8% fat. 263-280 Calories per pint with some loss in fat soluble vitamins.

Availability:

All year, sold in bottles with Red/Silver striped top and disposable containers.

Commodities — Dairy Products

Skimmed milk
Description:
Homogenised and pasteurised with most of the fat removed. Less than 0.3% fat. 195 Calories.

Availability:
All year, sold in bottles with blue silver checked top and disposable containers.

Sterilised milk
Description:
The milk is homogenised, bottled and sealed then heat treated to at least 100°C for 20-30 minutes and cooled. A slight caramel flavour. The sterilised process results in a loss of up to 35% Vitamin B1 (thiamin) and 50% B12.

Availability:
Sold in bottles with a long neck and crown caps and plastic bottles with blue caps. Skimmed or whole.

Ultra Heat Treated (UHT)
Other name: Long Life.
Description:
Homogenised milk is heated to not less than 132°C for 1 second then rapidly cooled and aseptically packed. Up to 60% B12 lost.

Dried whole milk powder
Description:
Contains all milk nutrients except Vitamin C, thiamin and Vitamin B12. These are destroyed by heat.

Availability:
All year, in powder form.

Dried skimmed milk
Description:
Contains virtually no fat.
Availability:
All year, in powder form.

Dried filled milk powder
Description:
Skimmed milk powder with added vegetable fat.
Availability:
All year.

Condensed milk
Description:
Made from whole or partly skimmed or skimmed milk. The milk is homogenised. Cane sugar is added. Evaporation at a temperature of +50°C to a concentration of 2.5 times the original.

Availability:
All year sold in cans.

Commodities — Dairy Products

Evaporated milk
Description:
Evaporated as for condensed milk without the addition of sugar to a concentration of 2 times the original.

Availability:
All year, sold in cans.

Butter milk
Description:
The liquid produced as a by-product of butter manufacture. It contains some protein, milk sugar and minerals.

Availability:
All year, in special shops.

Lactic Butter
Description:
A strong flavour of butter achieved by storing the cream at a temperature between 10-20°C, depending on the flavour required before churning.

Availability:
All year.

Butter (sweet)
Description:
A mild butter made by storing the cream at 4.5°C until the fat hardens.

Availability:
All year.

Cheese
Most English and foreign cheeses are made by clotting milk with an enzyme called rennin obtained from calves stomachs.

The old traditional methods of clotting milk using the juice of dandelions and thistles has been updated to make Vegetarian cheese by using Fungal Enzymes and Moulds such as:
  Mucor Miehei
  Mucor Pusillus Lindt
  Endthia Parasitica
  Bacillus Parasitica

A range of cheeses such as Cheddar and Cheshire are produced using these moulds.

Cottage cheese is made without a clotting agent. *Quark* and some cream cheeses use a small amount of rennin.

Commodities — Dairy Products

Half Cream
Description:
12% fat. Homogenised and may be UHT and pasteurised.
Availability:
All year, sold in cartons.

Single Cream
Description:
18% fat. Homogenised and pasteurised.
Availability:
All year, sold in cartons and bulk quantities.

Soured Cream
Description:
18% fat. Pasteurised and homogenised. Soured by the addition of lactic acid 'starter' culture.
Availability:
All year, sold in cartons.

Whipping Cream
Description:
35% fat. Pasteurised or UHT.
Availability:
All year, sold in cartons and packs.

Double Cream
Description:
48% fat. Slightly homogenised then pasteurised.
Availability:
All year, sold in cartons and bulk quantities.

Clotted Cream
Description:
55% fat. Heated to 82°C and cooled for about 4½ hours. In farm-produced cream the crust is left on, bulk quantities have the crust removed.
Availability:
All year, sold in cartons and trays.

Sterilised Half Cream
Description:
12% fat. Homogenised, filled into cans, sealed and heated to 108°C for at least 45 minutes and cooled rapidly.
Availability:
All year, sold in cans.

Sterilised Cream
Description:
23% fat. Processed as for sterilised half cream.
Availability:
All year.

Commodities — Dairy Products

Aerosol Cream
Description:
UHT cream in aerosol cans with Nitrous oxide as the propellant.

UHT Cream
Description:
Homogenised and heated to 140°C for at least 2 seconds. Cooled immediately.
Availability:
All year.

Additives
Caterer's and confectionery cream may have up to 13% sugar added. These creams may also contain a combined total of 0.3% stabilisers made up of a combination of:
- Sodium alginate
- Sodium carboxmethyl cellulose
- Carrageean
- Gelatine.

YOGHURT
1. The milk is pasteurised and cooled to 38°C.
2. It is inoculated with a mixed culture of Lactobacillus Bulgaricus and Streptococcus Thermophilus and incubated at 43°C. Sugar Lactose is fermented to Lactic Acid.
3. Incubation is continued until the acidity increases to the point where the milk protein Casein is precipitated and the product thickens.
4. Cooling to 4.5°C arrests the growth.
5. Fruit and flavour are stirred in.

Set-type
Description:
Stir-type yoghurt made with cow's or ewe's milk. Hung to remove surplus liquid and produce a thick cream-like consistency.

Stir-type
Description:
Incubated in large tanks and continually stirred to give a smooth cream-like consistency.

Greek
Description:
Incubated in the carton.

Commodities — Dried Fruits

Dried Fruits

Apricot
Other Names: (Prunus armeniaca).
Description: Origin, thought to be China. Arrived in this country during the 1560's. There are four types available: whole sulphured with a good orange colour and no stone, small whole non sulphured with a brownish colour, sulphured and half sun-dried.
Area of Production: California, Far East, Australia and Mediterranean countries.
Availability: All year round.

Bananas
Other Names: (Musa spp).
Description: Dried when fully ripe by sun drying.
Area of Production: Far East, Africa.
Availability: All year round.

Currants
Other Names: (Vitis vinifera).
Description: Small, round seedless grapes with thin skins. Dried in the sun on the ground by frequent turning. The smaller the currant the better.
Area of Production: Australia, Greece.
Availability: All year.

Commodities — Dried Fruits

Dates
Other Names: (Phoenix daetylifera).
Description: Thestoned product is half-dried in its tree before harvest but sun-dried whole dates are available. Very high in sugar.
Area of Production: Mediterranean countries and Middle East.
Availability: All year.

Figs
Other Names: (Ficus carvica).
Description: Originating in the Far East. The fig is a flower inside-out with its own fly to pollinate it.
Area of Production: Mediterranean countries, the best coming from Izmir in Turkey.
Availability: All year. Sun and oven dried.

Prune
Other Names: (Prunus demesticus var. Juliana).
Description: A variety of plum sulphured and dried.
Area of Production: California, Spain.
Availability: All year. Sold by count per kilo 65/70 50/60, 30/40 being its largest.

Commodities — Dried Fruits/Edible Fungi

Raisins
Other Names: (Vitis vinifera).
Description: A variety of usually seedless grape, either dried on its vine or on the ground by the sun. Artificial heat can be used. Aesthetic dressing (to prevent sugar crystals forming) of olive oil or liquid parafin or vegetable oil may be used.
Area of Production: The small dark seedless raisins are from Afghanistan and grown organically. Thompson seedless raisins are plump and juicy from California. Malaga large raisins from Spain, Lexia and Muscat from Australia.
Availability: All year.

Sultanas
Other Names: (Vitis vinifera).
Description: Light coloured seedless grape, sulphured.
Area of Production: Turkey and Australia.
Availability: All year.

Edible Fungi

Cep
Other Names: (Boletus edulis).
Description: Cap, brown, dry and smooth. 5 to 15cm across with yellow to brown pores and short bulging stem.
Area of Growth: Beech wood clearings
Availability: Fresh from August to November.

21

Commodities — Edible Fungi

Chanterelle
Other Names: (Cantharellus cibarius).
Description: Shaped like a funnel, egg-yolk in colour, up to 25cm across.
Area of Growth: Most woodlands.
Availability: Fresh from July to December.

Chinese Mushrooms
Description: There are two types: Winter/Fragrant which grows on trees or Straw Mushrooms that are grown on straw.
Availability: Both are available in dried and tinned form.

Button Mushrooms
Other Names: (Agaricus campestris).
Description: Cap, white open 1-10cm across with pink to brown gills.
Area of Growth: Fields, meadows.
Availability: Fresh from August to November.

Horn of Plenty
Other Names: (Craterellus cornucopoides).
Description: Funnel-shaped, up to 12cm high brown to black in colour.
Area of Growth: Beech woods.
Availability: Fresh from August to November or dried.

Commodities — Edible Fungi

Flat Mushroom
Other Names: (Agaricus arvensis).
Description: Cap, 5-25cm across, white with greyish gills.
Area of Growth: As for Field Mushrooms.
Availability: As for Field Mushrooms.

Puffball giant
Other Names: (Lycoperdon giganteum).
Description: A spherical fungus 10-30cm across, smooth leathery white with no stalk. The flesh is white solid and similar to a sponge.
Area of Growth: Woods, fields and under hedges.
Availability: Fresh from August to October.

Morel
Other Names: (Morchella esculenta).
Description: Cap 3-7cm across 2-10cm high, resembles a light brown sponge.
Area of Growth: Fields and woods.
Availability: Dried.

Truffle
Other Names: (Tuber aestirum).
Description: Walnut shaped with a blackberry skin 2-10cm across. The flesh is brownish — black and solid.
Area of Growth: Underground, found by trained pigs or dogs, mostly in France.
Availability: Mostly tinned in UK.

Commodities — Grains & Flours

Grains and Flours

Barley 
Other Names: (Hardeuin vulgare). Pot Barley, Bere, Scotch or hulled barley.
Description: Small hard mid brown grain with the outermost husk removed.
Area of Production: Most temperate countries.
Availability: All year.

Pearl Barley 
Other Names: Polished Barley.
Description: Barley with the outer layer and germ removed.
Area of Production: As for Barley.
Availability: As for Barley.

Barley Malt 
Other Names: Malted Barley.
Description: Barley which has been allowed to germinate in order to convert the starchy Endosperm into the sugar maltose.
Area of Production: As for Barley.
Availability: As for Barley.

Buckwheat 
Other Names: (Fagopyrum esculenta) Saracen Corn
Description: The plant is not a grain but is closely related to Rhubarb. Small diamond shaped and mid brown in colour. If roasted its colour is dark brown and is called Kasha.
Area of Production: Russia and Asia.
Availability: All year.

Commodities — Grains & Flours

Maize 
Other Names: (Zea mays) Corn, Corn on the Cob, Corne, Popcorn.
Description: Bright yellow round corns clustered around a stalk (cob).
Area of Production: America, Europe.
Availability: All year, tinned and frozen.

Millet Common 
Other Names: Types: Bulrush, Finger, Great and Sorghum.
Description: Common Millet has a dense cluster of small bright yellow round seeds.
Area of Production: China, and Far East.
Availability: All year.

Oats 
Other Names: (Avena sativa).
Description: Small oval seeds, gold in colour.
Area of Production: Europe.
Availability: All year.

Rolled Oats 
Other Names: As for Oats.
Description: Steamed crushed oats, may be fortified by the addition of thiamin.
Area of Production: As for Oats.
Availability: As for Oats.

Rice 
Other Names: (Oryza sativa).
Description: Similar grain to Wheat that grows in mud.
Area of Production: Asia, Africa, America.
Availability: All year.

Commodities — *Grains & Flours*

Brown Rice
Other Names: As for Rice.
Description: Large and short grain rice with the very outer husk removed but the inner husk intact.
Area of Production: As for Rice.
Availability: As for Rice.

Converted Rice
Other Names: As for Rice.
Description: A brown rice that has been steamed and injected with vitamins, sold polished, with a superior flavour to other rice.
Area of Production: As for Rice.
Availability: As for Rice.

Basmati Rice
Other Names: As for Rice.
Description: Off-white medium length rice sold polished, with a superior flavour to other rice. Also available as a brown rice.
Area of Production: India.
Availability: All year.

Wild Rice
Other Names: (Zizania aquatica). Canada, India.
Description: Grows in ponds and lakes, long and slim. Brown to black in colour.
Area of Production: North America and Canada.
Availability: All year.

Commodities — Grains & Flours

Rye 
Other Names: (Secale cereale).
Description: Small dark brown seeds.
Area of Production: Europe, Russia, Turkey.
Availability: All year.

Wheat 
Other Names: (Triticum vulgare).
Description: Small mid brown grain. Winter Wheat is grown in Britain and Europe, Spring Wheat is grown in America, Spring Wheat is high in gluten, Winter Wheat low in gluten.
Area of Production: Europe, America, Canada, Russia.
Availability: All year.

Bulghur Wheat 
Other Names: As for Wheat, Bulgur, Burgul, Bulgar.
Description: Whole Wheat is parboiled, dried and then cracked between rollers.
Area of Production: Eastern Europe and Western Asia.
Availability: All year.

Couscous 
Other Names: None.
Description: Semolina coated with flour, looks similar to Bulgar Wheat.
Area of Production: North Africa, Europe.
Availability: All year.

Commodities — Grains & Flours

Semolina 
Other Names: None.
Description: The endosperm of the Wheat grain.
Area of Production: As for Wheat.
Availability: All year in medium and coarse grain.

Barley Flour 
Description: A low protein flour.
Area of Production: Great Britain.
Availability: All year.

Buckwheat Flour 
Description: Approximately 90% whole grain, ground to a fine dark brown flour high in protein with no gluten.
Area of Production: As for Buckwheat.
Availability: All year.

Gram Flour 
Other Names: Chick pea flour.
Description: Finely ground chick peas seived to produce a pale yellow flour high in protein.
Area of Production: As for chick peas.
Availability: All year from specialist shops.

Oats 
Other Names: Oat flour, oatmeal.
Description: High protein, high fat flour. Oatmeal is sold coarsely ground, finely ground, or very finely ground.
Area of Production: Great Britain.
Availability: All year.

Commodities — Grains & Flours

Maize
Other Names: Corn flour; maize flour; white maize flour
Description: Maize flour: contains approximately 55% whole maize to produce fine texture meal. White maize flour: a whiter and more refined maize flour. Cornflour: refined maize starch.
Area of Production: USA, Egypt, South America.
Availability: All year.

Rice Flour
Other Names: Ground Rice.
Description: Low gluten flour. Ground rice has a coarse texture.
Area of Production: As for Rice.
Availability: All year.

Rye
Other Names: Rye meal, rye flour.
Description: Low gluten. Rye flour contains approximately 65% whole grain finely ground. Ryemeal contains approximately 85% whole grain coarsely ground.
Area of Production: Europe, Russia, Turkey,
Availability: All year.

Soy
Other Names: Soya flour.
Description: High protein with no gluten, a fine yellow flour.
Area of Production: As for soya beans.
Availability: All year.

Commodities — Grains & Flours/Herbs

Wheat
Other Names: Strong flour, Durum wheat flour, wholemeal flour, brown flour, plain flour, self-raising flour, chapatti flour.
Description: Strong flour — Flour with a high protein content.
Wholemeal flour: Contains the whole wheat grain. Brown flour has not less than 0.6% crude fibre.
Plain flour: General purpose medium protein flour.
Self-raising: A plain flour with the addition of chemical raising agents.
Chapatti flour: A very fine wholemeal flour used to make Indian bread.
Durum wheat flour: Very high gluten flour used to make pasta, produced in Italy.
Area of Production: All year.

Herbs

Basil, Sweet
Other Names: (Ocymum basilicum).
Description: Annual height up to 40cm, with bright but pale green leaves that are spade-shaped. The flowers are small and cream.
Area of Production: Tropical Africa and Asia.
Availability: Fresh in summer or dried all year round.

Commodities — Herbs

Basil
Other Names: Dark Opal.
Description: Same as for Sweet Basil but with dark purple leaves.
Area of Production: Same as Sweet Basil.
Availability: Same as Sweet Basil.

Bay Sweet
Other Names: (Laurus nobilis).
Description: Evergreen, height up to 3 metres with dark green pointed leaves. The flowers are yellow with no petals.
Area of Production: Mediterranean, Europe.
Availability: Fresh or dried, all year round.

Borage
Other Names: (Borage officinalis).
Description: Annual, height up to 90cm with rough hairy ovate green leaves with a smell of cucumber. The flowers 2-3cm and light blue.
Area of Production: Mediterranean.
Availability: Fresh in summer.

Chervil
Other Names: (Chaerophyllum sativum).
Description: Annual, height up to 45cm with mid green fern-like leaves. The flowers are white on 7cm wide beads.
Area of Production: E. Europe and Asia.
Availability: Fresh in Summer.

Commodities — Herbs

Chives
Other Names: (Allium schoenoprasum).
Description: Perennial, height up to 45cm. A tufted, onion flavoured plant with tubular mid-green leaves. The flowers are dark mauve.
Area of Production: Britain and Europe.
Availability: Fresh in April to September and dried.

Coriander
Other Names: (Coriandrum sativum).
Description: Annual, height up to 30cm. A slender branched plant with feathery leaves and pinkish flowers.
Area of Production: South Europe.
Availability: Fresh in late summer.

Dill
Other Names: (Anethum graveolens).
Description: Annual, height up to 90cm. A slender plant with deep green leaves divided into narrow segments. The flowers are small and yellow.
Area of Production: Mediterranean.
Availability: Fresh in June to August and dried.

Fennel, Garden
Other Names: (Foeniculum vulgare).
Description: Perennial, height up to 90cm. The plant has branched feathery leaves and yellow flowers.
Area of Production: Britain, Europe.
Availability: Fresh in June to October and dried.

Commodities — Herbs

Garlic
Other Names: (Allium sativrum).
Description: Perennial, height up to 40cm. A bulb made up of small sections known as cloves.
Area of Production: Asia and Middle East.
Availability: Fresh from August, also as a paste and dried.

Hyssop
Other Names: (Hyssopus officinalis).
Description: Perennial, height up to 60cm with narrow mid-green leaves and blue/mauve flowers.
Area of Production: North and Central Europe.
Availability: Fresh June to September also dried.

Marjoram, pot
Other Names: (Origanum onites).
Description: Perennial, height up to 60cm with mid-green leaves and pinkish/mauve flowers.
Area of Production: Mediterranean.
Availability: Fresh July to September also dried.

Oregano
Other Names: Wild Marjoram (Origanum vulgare).
Description: Perennial, height up to 30cm with small mid-green leaves and purple flowers.
Area of Production: Britain and Europe.
Availability: Fresh July to September also dried.

Commodities — Herbs

Mint, Apple 
Other Names: Round Leaves (Mentha suaveolens).
Description: Perennial, height up to 60cm with pointed ovate green leaves. The flowers are small, white or cream.
Area of Production: Europe.
Availability: Fresh in summer.

Other Mints
Other Names: Ginger, Scotch, Eau de Cologne, Orange, Pineapple, Peppermint, Horsemint.

Spearmint 
Other Names: Garden Mint, Green Lamb Mint, Pea Mint (Mentha x spicata).
Description: Height up to 45cm with long ovate leaves. The flowers are small and lilac. The most common mint for culinary use.
Area of Production: Europe.
Availability: Fresh in summer, also dried.

Parsley 
Other Names: Curly (Petroselinum crispum).
Description: Biennial, height up to 20cm with tight curly leaves.
Area of Production: South Europe, mostly used in Britain.
Availability: Fresh in summer, also dried.

Commodities — Herbs

Parsley
Other Names: Hamburg or Turnip-rooted (Petroselinum crispin 'Tuberosum').
Description: Biennial, height up to 60cm with broad open curly leaves.
Area of Production: Developed for cultivation.
Availability: Fresh leaves summer, root in winter mostly used in Continental Europe.

Rosemary
Other Names: (Rosmarinus officinalis).
Description: Perennial, height up to 150cm, a bushy evergreen with narrow mid-green leaves on top, almost white beneath. The flowers are pale blue.
Area of Production: Mediterranean.
Availability: Fresh all year round, also dried.

Sage, Common
Other Names: (Salvia officinalis).
Description: Perennial, height up to 50cm. A bushy evergreen with pale grey-green ovate leaves. The flowers are purple or white.
Area of Production: North Mediterranean.
Availability: Fresh from June to November, also dried.

Savoury, Winter
Other Names: (Satureia montana).
Description: Perennial, height up to 45cm and looks like Summer Savoury with Pale Pink flowers.
Area of Production: South Europe.
Availability: Fresh in summer, also dried.

Commodities — Herbs/Nuts & Seeds

Sorrel
Other Names:	(Rumex acetosa).
Description:	Perennial, height up to 60cm with large spinach-like green leaves. The flowers are small and pink.
Area of Production:	Central Europe.
Availability:	Fresh in spring and summer.

Tarragon, French
Other Names:	(Artemisia dracunculus).
Description:	Perennial, height up to 90cm with narrow dark green leaves. Seldom flowers in Britain.
Area of Production:	Southern Europe.
Availability:	Fresh from June to November, also dried.

Thyme, Garden
Other Names:	(Thymus vulgaris).
Description:	Perennial, height up to 30cm with small mid-green leaves and purple flowers.
Area of Production:	Southern Europe.
Availability:	Fresh in summer, also dried.
Other Thymes:	Lemon, Caraway, Wild.

Nuts and Seeds

Brazil
Other Names:	(Bertholletia excelsa).
Description:	A large dark brown nut shaped like an orange segment. Approximately 14 nuts contained in one pod called Gourd.
Area of Production:	South America.
Availability:	All year whole, shelled.

Commodities — Nuts & Seeds

Cashew
Other Names: (Anacardium occidentale).
Description: Small 2cm kidney shaped nuts with a mild taste and cream colour.
Area of Production: Africa, South America, India.
Availability: All year, whole, shelled.

Sweet chestnut
Other Names: (Castanea vesca).
Description: Large hemi-sphere, dark brown in colour, grows two per green prickly fruit body.
Area of Production: Spain and Europe.
Availability: Fresh all year, dried, shelled.

Coconut
Other Names: (Cocos nucifera).
Description: Very large oval nut, covered with fibre. The kernels are used to make copra.
Area of Production: Tropical countries.
Availability: All year, fresh, dried, dessicated, powdered, flakes, creamed.

Hazelnuts
Other Names: (Corylus avellana). Cob, Filberts, Barcelona nuts.
Description: A hard light brown shell with parchment covered spherical nut. Depending on area of production, size and shape may change.
Area of Production: Europe and Middle East.
Availability: Fresh whole in Autumn, shelled all year.

Commodities — Nuts & Seeds

Macadamia Nut
Other Names: (Macadamia termifolia).
Description: Spherical with a very hard shell which varies in size.
Area of Production: Australia and Pacific Islands.
Availability: All year round.

Peanut
Other Names: (Arachis hypogae). Monkeynuts, Ground Nuts, Gubers.
Description: Small reddish legumes contained in a light brown underground root.
Area of Production: North America, South America.
Availability: All year whole, shelled, skinned, salted, ground as butter.

Pecan
Other Names: (Carglus rostrata).
Description: 2-3cm oval, smooth pale brown nut with a hard shell. The edible nut resembles a long walnut with a mild flavour.
Area of Production: North America.
Availability: All year whole or shelled.

Pine Nuts
Other Names: (Pinus pinea). India Nut, Pignalices.
Description: The small yellow seed of a species of Pine Tree.
Area of Production: Mediterranean Countries.
Availability: All year.

Commodities — Nuts & Seeds

Pistachio
Other Names: (Pistacia vera).
Description: 1cm oval, light brown shell with a slight split, brown greenish kernels, soft in texture with a mild flavour.
Area of Production: Middle East, North America.
Availability: All year whole and shelled.

Walnut
Other Names: (Juglans regia). English Walnut.
Description: 2-3cm smooth but irregular spherical hard shell with two kernels joined at the centre.
Area of Production: America (Black Walnuts), Europe, Mediterranean Countries.
Availability: All year shelled, whole winter.

Pumpkin seed
Other Names: (Cucurbita pepo).
Description: 5cm greenish oval flat seeds from the ground Pumpkin. Some seeds are sold without the hard outer green shell.
Area of Production: Europe, Asia, North America.
Availability: All year.

Sesame seeds
Other Names: (Sesamum indicum).
Description: Small brown seeds obtained from the pod of a herb.
Area of Production: Africa, Middle and Far East.
Availability: All year.

Commodities — Nuts & Seeds/Sea Vegetables

Sunflower seeds 
Other Names: (Helianthus annuus).
Description: The seed from the tall Sunflower. Small grey and soft, with a mild oil flavour.
Area of Production: Russia, North & South America, Europe.
Availability: All year used as oil seed.

Sweet Almonds 
Other Names: (Amygdalus communis).
Description: Sweet almonds as opposed to Bitter almonds are pale brown with a very hard outer shell and skin-like inner nut covering.
Area of Production: Mediterranean countries eg: Italy also West Coast of USA.
Availability: All year, whole, shelled, blanched, split, nib, ground, flake.

Sea Vegetables

Agar 
Other Names: Agar-Agar.
Description: A gelatine substitute made from various gelatinous species.
Area of Production: World wide.
Availability: All year in flakes or powder.

Arame 
Other Names: (Eisenia arbovea). Sea Oak, Southern Sea Palm.
Description: Brown broad leaf when fresh.
Area of Production: Pacific coasts.
Availability: Dried black in colour, cut into fine strips.

Commodities — Sea Vegetables

Carrageen
Other Names: (Chandrus crispus). Irish Moss.
Description: Red algae, 7-10cm branched fronds, light brown when dried.
Area of Production: Atlantic coast.
Availability: All year.

Dulse
Other Names: (Rhodymenia palmata).
Description: Purplish-red, 1-5cm wide strips.
Area of Production: Atlantic and Pacific, Far North and South.
Availability: All year.

Laver
Other Names: (Porphyra umbilicalis). Laverbread.
Description: Broad red-purple fronds but can also be green in colour. (Ulva-lactuca) or Sea Lettuce. Red considered best.
Area of Production: World wide in cold waters.
Availability: All year.

Hijiki
Other Names: (Hizikia fusifrome).
Description: Small fronds.
Area of Production: Far East and Japan.
Availability: All year, dried.

Commodities — Sea Vegetables

Kombu
Other Names: (Laminaria japonica).
Description: Blackish brown when fresh, grey brown flat strips when dried.
Area of Production: Japan.
Availability: All year, dried.

Nori
Other Names: (Porphyra-teneva).
Description: Broad green leaves when fresh, light brown when dried, similar to laver.
Area of Production: Japan.
Availability: All year dried.

Marah Samphire
Other Names: (Salicomia europaea). Samphire.
Description: Small 10-15cm green branching cactus-like plant.
Area of Production: East coast of Britain between tides on flat beaches.
Availability: Early summer.

Wakame
Other Names: (Undaria pinnatifida).
Description: Broad grey-brownish strips when dry.
Area of Production: Japan, Far East.
Availability: All year dried.

Commodities — Soya Products

Soya Products

Miso
Other Names: Shaikyo (white), Mugi (Barley based), Hatche, Mame, Genmai and Kome (Rice based).
Description: Soya beans are soaked and fermented in some cases with Brown Rice and Barley for periods of up to 3 years. This produces 4 basic types: white, sweet, salty, red.
Area of Production: Japan, China (Chiang).
Availability: All year — most common in UK, Hatcho, Mugi, Genmai.

Okara
Other Names: Soya husk.
Description: The remains from making soya milk.
Area of Production: Where Tofu and milk are made.
Availability: Usually made as a by product.

Tamari
Other Names: None.
Description: A liquid made darker and stronger than Soya sauce.
Area of Production: Japan.
Availability: All year.

Commodities — Soya Products

Tempeh
Other Names: None.
Description: A fermented soya cheese made by mixing soya beans with a mould called Rhizopus oligosporus.
Area of Production: Indonesia, UK.
Availability: All year in special shops.

Tofu
Other Names: Bean Curd.
Description: Curdled Soya Milk using Nigari or Epsom Salts to make the milk curdle.
Area of Production: Far East, Europe.
Availability: Silken (soft), Regular (firm), Smoked regular.

Shoyu
Other Names: None.
Description: Traditionally made Soya sauce fermented up to 2 years.
Area of Production: Japan, China, Europe.
Availability: All year.

T.V.P. Textured Vegetable Protein
Other Names: None.
Description: High protein food made by extruding vegetable protein in particular soya bean.
Area of Production: UK and USA.
Availability: All year.

Commodities — Spices

Spices

Allspice
Other Names: Pimento Berries, Myrtle Pepper (Pimenta officinalis).
Description: The unripe dried fruits of a small tree with oblong narrow leaves and clusters of tiny white flowers.
Area of Production: West Indies and South America.
Availability: As berries and powder.

Anise
Other Names: Sweet Cumin (Pimpinella anisum).
Description: The dried ripe fruit of an annual herb with fern like leaves. The flowers are yellowish to white but the plant rarely fruits in Britain.
Area of Production: East Mediterranean.
Availability: As seed or powder.

Anise
Other Names: Star, Chinese Anise (Illicium verum).
Description: The star-like dried seeds of a small evergreen tree with ovate leaves and yellow flowers.
Area of Production: South West China.
Availability: As stars or powder.

Commodities — Spices

Asafoetida
Other Names: Asafetida or Food of the Gods (Ferula assa-foetida).
Description: The gum-resin obtained from a species of fennel-giant. The latex is tapped from the root of plants that have not flowered, often mixed with gypsum, gum arabic or flour.
Area of Production: Afghanistan.
Availability: As powder, lumps or flakes.

Caraway
Other Names: (Carum carvi).
Description: A biennial herb growing up to 90cm with feathery leaves and small white flowers.
Area of Production: Asia Minor.
Availability: As seed or powder.

Cardamoms
Other Names: Malabar Cardamons (Elettaria, cardamomum).
Description: Two main types: Bleached or Green. The fleached are yellow to cream or brown to black seeds, shaped like small round pips. The Green are dried washed fruits shaped like pale green orange pips or melon pips, both from a reed like plant with yellowish flowers.
Area of Production: South India and Sri-Lanka.
Availability: As seeds or powder.

Commodities — Spices

Cayenne
Other Names: Bird pepper (Capsicum annuum).
Description: A small shrub approximately 100cm high, ovate leaves and white flowers. The fruits are 5 to 10cm long, bright red in colour when ripe and filled with yellow seeds.
Area of Production: South America.
Availability: Fresh, dried or powder.

Celery Seed
Other Names: Smallage Seed (Apium graveolens).
Description: Small brown seeds from the common garden celery.
Area of Production: Europe.
Availability: Dried as seeds or powder.

Chilli
Other Names: Spur Pepper (Capiscum frutescens) other spellings: Chilly, Chile, Chili.
Description: A shrub with ovate leaves and greenish-white flowers. The fruit is bright red in colour 3-10cm long.
Area of Production: South America.
Availability: Fresh, dried, powdered.

Commodities — Spices

Cinnamon
Other Names: (Cinnamomum zeylanicum).
Description: The dried inner bark of a species of Laurel tree. The tree is pollarded to produce young shoots which are stripped of their bark, curled and dried in 'quills'. The quills are then cut into small lengths.
Area of Production: South India and Sri-Lanka.
Availability: Quills, powdered, mixed with sugar.

Cloves
Other Names: (Eugenia caryophyllata).
Description: The sun-dried unopened flowerbuds of a small evergreen plant.
Area of Production: Malluca Islands, Zanzibar.
Availability: Whole, powdered.

Coriander
Other Names: Chinese Parsley (Coriandrum sativum).
Description: Height up to 60cm with pinkish-white flowers. The leaves are used as a herb. The seeds are yellowish-brown in colour.
Area of Production: Middle and Far East.
Availability: Whole or powdered.

Commodities — Spices

Cumin
Other Names: (Cuminum cyminum).
Description: Height up to 30cm an annual plant with a cone shape. The leaves are pale green and the flowers are white to pink.
Area of Production: Middle and Far East.
Availability: Whole or powdered.

Dill Seeds
Other Names: (Peucedanum graveolens).
Description: The seeds of the herb Dill.
Area of Production: Mediterranean.
Availability: Whole or powdered.

Fennel Seeds
Other Names: (Foeniculum vulgare).
Description: The seeds of Garden Fennel.
Area of Production: Britain, Europe.
Availability: Whole or powdered.

Ginger
Other Names: (Zingiber officinale).
Description: A perennial plant with thick knobbly rhizomes and large light green leaves. The flowers are yellowish-white with a black and yellow marbled lip.
Area of Production: Far East.
Availability: Fresh or dried as a powder or whole.

Commodities — Spices

Mace 
Other Names: (Myristica fragrans).
Description: The yellow covering of the Nutmeg situated between the outer husk and the nutmeg. From an evergreen tree called Myristica fragrans.
Area of Production: Molucca Islands.
Availability: As blades or powdered.

Mustard, three types 
Other Names: Black (Brassica nigra), White (Brassica arvensis), Brown (Brassica juncea).
Description: Both black and white seeds are used in mustard powder. The black seeds give aroma and the white strength. Brown seeds are used in some curry powders and called Rai.
Area of Production: Black and White: European; Brown: Far East.
Availability: Seeds or powder.

Nutmeg 
Other Names: (Myristica fragrans).
Description: See Mace.
Area of Production: See Mace.
Availability: See Mace.

Commodities — Spices

Paprika
Other Names: (Capsicum annuum).
Description: A reddish-brown powder obtained from dried sweet capsicums or peppers.
Area of Production: Central America.
Availability: As powder.

Pepper
Other Names: Black, White, Green (Piper nigrum).
Description: A vine-like herb which climbs trees. It has dark green leaves and small yellowish-green flowers. The fruit hangs in bright red clusters when fully ripe. Green pepper corns are the unripe berries sold in tins or jars of water. Black pepper corns are picked when green and fermented in heaps then dried. White pepper corns are picked when nearly ripe then soaked in water to remove the outer skin, then dried.
Area of Production: India.
Availability: Powder, all year.

Saffron
Other Names: (Crocus sativus).
Description: The hand picked stigmas of a perennial crocus with violet flowers.
Area of Production: Asia-Minor, Spain.
Availability: In small packets of dried stigma.

51

Commodities — Spices

Sesame
Other Names: (Sesamum indicum).
Description: Grows up to 2m in height with variable leaves and white or pink flowers.
Area of Production: Middle and Far East.
Availability: Seeds.

Turmeric
Other Names: (Curcuma longa).
Description: A perennial herb up to 60cm high, a member of the Ginger family. The rhizomes, which are bright orange-yellow inside, are boiled and sun dried. Only the best 'fingers' are ground.
Area of Production: Southern Asia.
Availability: Powdered.

Vanilla
Other Names: (Vanilla planifolia).
Description: The unripe fruit pods of a climbing orchid with long wide bright green leaves and pale green flowers.
Area of Production: Central America.
Availability: As pods or essence; most essence is made from the oil of cloves.

CHAPTER 3
Basic Preparations

Many of the basic preparations shown in this chapter apply to all types of catering but to satisfy the principles of vegetarianism and healthy eating certain adaptations have been made to meet this need. Some of the basic preparations have been adapted by using non animal ingredients or expanded to be more versatile in their use. There are also some which are solely vegetarian in their make up and use. These preparations have been categorised into pastries, stocks, sauces, dressings, creams and batters.

It must be emphasised that these preparations are not presented as dishes in themselves but as a basic part of a given meal or dish, or in some cases as an accompaniment to one.

The basic preparations explained in this chapter have, for easy reference purposes been grouped as follows:

Grains & Pulses
Cooking of Grains
Preparation and Cooking of Pulses
Tofu

Pastries
Sweet Short Wholemeal Pastry
Savoury Short Wholemeal Pastry
Wholemeal Hot Water Pastry
Wholemeal Puff Pastry
Wholemeal Choux Pastry
Vegetarian Suet Pastry
Fillo Pastry
Noodle Pastry

Stocks & Sauces
Basic White Stock
Basic Brown Stock
Stock Concentrate
Basic Savoury White Sauce
Basic Sweet White Sauce
Basic White Stock Sauce
Basic Brown Sauce
Basic Warm Sauces
Basic Cheese Sauce
White Vegetable Sauces
Vegetable Sauces
Sweet and Sour Mushroom

Basic Preparations — Grains & Pulses

Dressings
Basic Oil and Vinegar Dressing
Mayonnaise
Vegan Mayonnaise — Cocktail Sauce
Yoghurt Dressing
Pesto — Pesto Dressing
Cashewnut and Gooseberry Dressing
Nut Creams

Batters
Light Crispy Batter
Pancake Batter
Blini
Croutons

Grains & Pulses
Cooking of Grains, Preparation and Cooking of Pulses, Tofu

Cooking Grains

Process
Buckwheat
1. Cook one part buckwheat in two parts liquid.
2. Bring to the boil and cook for 12 minutes in the oven at moderate temperature.

Basmati Rice
1. Soak the rice in cold water for one hour and then drain.
2. Cook one part rice in one part liquid.
3. Bring to the boil and cook for 20 minutes in the oven.

Brown Rice, Braised
1. Cook one part rice in two parts liquid.
2. Bring to the boil, cover and cook in the oven for 40-50 minutes.

Brown Rice, Boiled
1. Cook one part in three parts liquid.
2. Bring to the boil and simmer for 40-50 minutes.

White Rice, Braised
1. Cook one part rice in two parts liquid.
2. Bring to the boil, cover and cook for 20 minutes in the oven.

54

Basic Preparations — Grains & Pulses

White Rice, Boiled
1. Cook one part rice in three parts liquid.
2. Bring to the boil and simmer for 20 minutes.

Wild Rice
1. Place in boiling water, remove from the heat and soak for an hour and then drain.
2. Cook one part rice in three parts liquid.
3. Bring to the boil and cook for 45 minutes in the oven.

Millet
1. Cook one part millet in three parts liquid.
2. Bring to the boil and cook for 12 minutes in the oven.

Wheat, Rye, Oats, Barley
1. Cook one part grain in two parts liquid.
2. Bring to the boil and cook for 70-80 minutes in the oven.

Preparation & Cooking of Pulses

For the purposes of hygiene, it is unwise to assume that any pulse or legume is clean. They should be washed in running cold water and picked over to remove grit and stones and any that are discoloured.

Cold Soaking
It is not necessary to soak lentils, but peas and beans must be soaked for at least 12 hours and a minimum of 5 hours.

Once washed and picked over, place the beans or peas in a bowl of at least twice their volume to allow for expansion. Cover with plenty of cold water and place a lid or cling film over the container to protect from dust. Soaking beans are best stored in a cool place or refrigerator to prevent any fermentation.

Cooking
Having soaked the pulses as necessary, drain and rinse under running cold water to remove all the soaking water.

Place the pulses in a saucepan capable of holding twice their volume and cover with cold water.

Bring to the boil and hold at a rapid boil for at least 10 minutes in order to destroy toxins which are present in pulses like kidney beans. Set to simmer, removing any scum that rises to the surface, until the pulses are just soft when pressed between finger and thumb. At this stage, salt and any other flavouring ingredients are added (adding salt at the start of cooking toughens the pulses, prolonging the cooking time).

Continue simmering until the pulses are completely soft, along with any vegetables that may have been added with the salt.

When cooked, pulses may be stored in a refrigerator or deep frozen with a little of the cooking liquid.

If the pulses are for salads they should be drained and while still hot a marinade added. Cold pulses will not absorb so much flavour.

Tofu

Ingredients
- 150mls Uncooked soya beans.
- 5g Epsom salts or lemon juice ½-1 lemon or 4g ngari.
- 300mls Cold water.   1.5l   Boiling water.

Process
1. Soak the soya beans overnight.
2. Blend soaked beans with 300mls of water to make GO.
3. Add GO to 1.25l of boiling water in a large pan. Stir to boil, cool with cold water, reboil, repeat 3 times.
4. Strain through muslin, to produce soya milk and okara soy bran.
5. Bring soya milk back to the boil.
6. Dissolve Ngari or epsom salts in water.
7. Add salts or lemon juice to boiling milk *off boil.*
8. *Do not stir* — allow to stand to produce a greenish whey & tofu.
9. Remove the whey by straining.
10. Press the curds (tofu) to give hard tofu about 2 hours.
11. To keep — put under cold water, change water every day.

Basic Preparations — Pastries

Pastries

Wholemeal Puff Pastry, Wholemeal Hot Water Pastry, Noodle Pastry, Sweet Short Wholemeal Pastry, Savoury Short Wholemeal Pastry, Wholemeal Choux Pastry, Vegetarian Suet Pastry, Fillo Pastry.

Wholemeal Puff Pastry

Yield — 500g

Ingredients

500g	Wholemeal flour.
	Pinch salt.
	Pinch cream of tartar.
60g	Vegetarian margarine.
260-310g	Water.
315g	Hard vegetarian margarine or butter.

Process
1. Make a dough with the first five ingredients.
2. Roll the dough out into a rectangle.
3. Cover two thirds of the rectangle with the butter or hard margarine.
4. Fold into three (½ a turn).
5. Roll out along the length to the original size.
6. Repeat stage no. 4 of the process to give two more ½ turns.
7. Place in a refrigerator for 10 minutes.
8. Remove from the refrigerator and give two more ½ turns.
9. Place in the refrigerator for 20 minutes.
10. Remove from the refrigerator and give 1½ turns.
11. Store in the refrigerator or, if to be used immediately, give 2 more ½ turns. Dust with bran as necessary.

Basic Preparations — Pastries

Wholemeal Hot Water Pastry

Yield — 450g

Ingredients
- 450g Wholemeal flour.
- 180ml Water.
- 110g Hard vegetable fat.
- 3g   Salt.

Process
1. Place the water, fat and salt in a saucepan and bring to the boil.
2. Place the flour in a large basin.
3. Add the boiling liquid to the flour and work with a spoon into a rough dough.
4. As soon as the temperature will allow, work by hand into a smooth paste.
5. *Use while still hot* as the cold paste is very difficult to work.

Noodle Pastry

Yield — 200g

Ingredients
- 175g Strong wholemeal flour.
- 50ml Water *or* egg yolks and 20mls water *or* 1 egg yolk and 100g cooked spinach *or* 1 egg yolk and 30mls tomato puree.
- 10ml Olive oil.
- Sea salt and freshly ground nutmeg.

Process
1. Combine all ingredients to make a soft but not sticky dough.
2. Rest for 1 hour.
3. Roll out as required — keeping dough covered with a damp cloth.

Basic Preparations — Pastries

Sweet Short Wholemeal Pastry

Yield — 400g

Ingredients

- 400g Wholemeal flour.
- 195g Vegetarian fat.
- 45g   Brown sugar.
- 2.5g Salt.
- 65g   Water.

Process
1. Work the dry ingredients and fat to a crumble texture.
2. Add the water and mix to a paste.
3. Store in a refrigerator before use.

Savoury Short Wholemeal Pastry

Yield — 400g

Ingredients

- 145g Wholemeal flour.
- 85g   Vegetarian fat.
- 30g   Vegetarian margarine.
- 145g Wholemeal flour.
- 2.5g Baking powder.
- 2.5g Salt.
- 75g   Water.

Process
1. Cream the first three ingredients together.
2. Add the second three ingredients and work to a crumble texture.
3. Add the water and mix to a paste.
4. Store in a refrigerator before use.

Basic Preparations — Pastries

Wholemeal Choux Pastry

Yield — 400ml

Ingredients
- 135g   Wholemeal flour.
- 160ml Water.
- 80g   Butter or vegetable margarine.
- 150g   Beaten eggs.

Process
1. Boil the water and fat in a small saucepan.
2. Add the flour and work off the heat until a smooth paste is formed.
3. Allow the paste to go cold as a warm paste will make the egg cook.
4. Work the eggs into the cool paste one by one until a smooth dropping consistency is reached.
5. Use as required.

Vegetarian Suet Pastry

Yield — 200g

Ingredients
- 200g   Wholemeal flour.
- 100g   Vegetable suet.
- 100ml Cold water.
- 5g   Sea salt.
- 6g   Baking powder.

Process
1. Work the dry ingredients and fat to a crumble texture.
2. Add the water and mix to a dough.

Basic Preparations — Pastries

Fillo Pastry

Yield — 400g

Ingredients
- 75g   Corn flour.
- 325g   Strong unbleached flour *or* 150g Wholewheat strong flour *mixed with* 150g Unbleached strong flour.
- 240ml Water.
- 10ml   Corn oil.

Process
1. Thoroughly mix the flours.
2. Make a well, add half the water and mix. Then add the remaining half.
3. Cover with a damp cloth and allow to rest for 1-1½ hours.
4. Cut into eight pieces and roll each piece out until it is very thin.
5. Keep the remaining dough covered.
6. Cover the rolled pastry until it is to be used.

Basid Preparations — Stock & Sauces

Stocks & Sauces

Basic Stocks — Basic White Stock, Basic Brown Stock, Stock Concentrate, Basic Sauces — Basic Savoury White Sauce, Basic Sweet White Sauce, Basic White Stock Sauce, Basic Brown Sauce, Basic Warm Sauces, White Vegetable Sauces, Vegetable Sauces — Tomato, Spinach, Red Pepper, Basic Cheese Sauce, Sweet and Sour Mushroom

Basic Stocks

Yield — 1 litre

Basic White Stock
Yield — 1 litre
Ingredients

2l	Water.		**Seasoning**
100g	Carrot	2	Sprigs thyme
75g	Celery.	½	Clove garlic (optional)
100g	Leek.	1	Bay leaf
75g	Onion.	4	Parsley stalks
1tsp	Cold pressed sunflower oil.	1	Sprig rosemary.

Basic Brown Stock
Yield — 1 litre
Ingredients

2l	Water.		**Seasoning**
50g	Mushrooms.	2	Sprigs thyme
75g	Carrot.	¼	Clove garlic.
75g	Celery.	¼	Bay leaf.
75g	Leek.	2	Parsley stalks.
75g	Onion.	1	Pinch oregano.
50g	Tomatoes.		
1tsp	Cold pressed sunflower oil.		

Basic Preparations — Stocks/Sauces

Process
1. Clean all the vegetables and peel where necessary.
2. Cut the prepared vegetables into small roughly shaped dice.
3. Heat the oil in a 3 litre saucepan.
4. For Brown Stock, fry all vegetables, except mushrooms, garlic and tomatoes, until golden brown.
   For White Stock, sweat all vegetables without colour.
5. Add water and the remaining ingredients.
6. Simmer for 45 minutes, skimming as scum forms on the top.
7. Strain.
8. Reduce to 1 litre.

NOTE: For Brown Stock shoyu and tamari may be added to increase the flavour and colour.

Stock Concentrate

Stock concentrate is made by reducing 5 litres of basic Brown stock to 500ml.

Process
During the reduction process the stock must be strained through a fine conical strainer into a shallow pan just big enough to contain the amount of liquid at that time. This process is continued until the desired amount is reached.

The constant straining of the liquid will remove unwanted vegetable fibre leaving a thick black flavoursome paste.

Stock concentrate can be used to replace bought stock cubes or to enhance the flavour of other stocks, soups and sauces.

Basic Preparations — Stocks/Sauces

Basic Sauces

Yield — 1 litre

Basic Savoury White Sauce
Yields — 1 litre
- 100g Butter or vegetable margarine.
- 100g Wholemeal flour or unbleached flour.
- 1   Onion studded with 1 clove.
- 1l   Milk or soya milk.

Basic Sweet White Sauce
Yields — 1 litre
- 100g Butter or vegetable margarine.
- 100g Wholemeal flour or unbleached flour.
- 1l   Milk or soya milk.
- 50g   Castor sugar.

Basic White Stock Sauce
Yields — 1 litre
- 100g Butter or vegetable margarine.
- 100g Wholemeal flour or unbleached flour.
- 1l   Basic white stock.

Basic Brown Stock Sauce
Yields — 1 litre
- 100g Butter or vegetable margarine.
- 100g Wholemeal flour.
- 1l   Double reduced brown stock.

Basic Preparations — Stocks/Sauces

Process
1. Melt the fat in a thick bottomed saucepan.
2. Add the flour.
3. a) For basic white sauce, cook over a gentle heat until the mixture turns sandy in texture.
   b) For basic white stock sauce, cook over gentle heat until the mixture has a slight colour.
   c) For basic brown stock sauce, cook over gentle heat until the mixture has turned an even light brown colour.
4. Draw the saucepan to a cool part of the stove and add a small amount of the liquid.
5. Stir with a non metal spoon over the heat until a smooth paste is produced.
6. Add more liquid, repeating the process until all the liquid has been used.
7. Simmer in the oven or on top of the stove for one hour.
8. To finish the sweet sauce, add the sugar and work to dissolve.
9. Cover the surface with melted fat to prevent a skin forming. Use as required.

Other White Vegetables' Sauces

Yield — 1 Litre

Ingredients
- 1 litre Basic white sauce.
- 50g Grated vegetarian cheese.
- 100g Cooked, puréed vegetable; fennel or onion or celery or white of leek.

Process
1. Reheat the basic white sauce.
2. Stir in the puréed vegetable and cheese.
3. Reboil and cool.

Basic Preparations — Stocks/Sauces

Basic Warm Sauces

Yield — 0.5 Litres

Bearnaise

Ingredients
- 50g   Shallots.
- 10   White pepper corns.
- 6   Egg yolks.
- 500g   Clarified butter.
- 1g   Ground sea salt.
-        Pinch Cayenne pepper.
- 15ml   Lemon juice.
- 40ml   Tarragon vinegar.
- 2g   Chopped tarragon.

Hollandaise

Ingredients
- 50g   Shallots.
- 10   White pepper corns.
- 6   Egg yolks.
- 500g   Clarified butter.
- 1g   Ground sea salt.
-        Pinch Cayenne pepper.
- 15ml   Lemon juice.
- 20ml   Cold water.

Process
1. Peel and finely chop the shallots.
2. a) For Hollandaise: in a shallow pan sweat the shallots and corns.
   b) For Bearnaise: reduce in shallow pan the shallots, pepper corns and tarragon vinegar.
3. Remove from the heat.
4. Add the egg yolks.
5. Over a bath of hot water whisk the mixture until a thick creamy consistency when a figure of eight can be drawn with ribbon from the whisk, using a high and low heat the correct consistency has been reached. Do not over-heat as the egg will scramble.
6. Remove from the heat.
7. Whilst whisking continuously, slowly add the warm clarified butter. Do not add the white whey.
8. Strain to remove shallots and pepper corns.
9. a) For Hollandaise: finish to taste with lemon juice and cayenne pepper.
   b) For Bearnaise: finish to taste with lemon juice and chopped tarragon.
10. Correct the consistency with water if necessary.

Basic Preparations — Stocks/Sauces

Vegetable Sauces

Yield — 500ml

Tomato Sauce

Ingredients

500g	Fresh tomatoes.
10mls	Tomato puree.
25g	Finely chopped shallots.
40mls	White vegetable stock.
1	Clove crushed garlic.
	Sea salt and freshly ground black pepper.

Seasoning

Pinch of dried Basil *or*
Sprig fresh basil.
Sprig Thyme.

Spinach Sauce

Ingredients

400g	Cooked spinach.
100mls	White vegetable stock.
100mls	Greek yoghurt or double cream.
	Sea salt and freshly ground pepper.

Process
1. Wash and prepare vegetables.
2. a) *For green vegetables*: blanch in boiling salted water or steam until just cooked and refresh in cold water.
   b) *For other vegetables*: sweat in vegetable stock or oil.
3. Add remaining stock and herbs.
4. Simmer until cooked.
5. Remove herbs.
6. Liquidise.
7. Re-boil and correct seasoning and consistency.
8. May be finished with yoghurt or double cream.

Basic Preparations — Stocks/Sauces

Variations to Hollandaise
1. *Pepper sauce:* add finely chopped green and red peppers to the finished sauce.
2. *Maltaise sauce:* add orange juice and blanched strips of orange zest to finished sauce.
3. *Curry:* add cooked curry powder and a fine dice of red pepper.

Variations to Bearnaise.
1. *Choron sauce:* add tomato purée or a purée of fresh uncooked tomatoes to finish sauce.

Red Pepper Sauce

Yield — 500ml

Ingredients
- 500ml Vegetable stock.
- 50g   Finely chopped onion.
- 10g   Paprika.
- 30ml   Olive oil.
-        Sea salt and freshly ground black pepper.
- 500g   Red peppers finely diced.

Process
1. Fry the paprika in the olive oil.
2. Add the red peppers and onions and sweat until soft.
3. Add the stock, re-boil and simmer until cooked.
4. Liquidise.
5. Re-boil and correct seasoning and consistency.

Basic Preparations — Stocks/Sauces

Cheese Sauce

Yield — 1 Litre

Ingredients
- 1 litre Basic white sauce.
- 150g Grated vegetarian cheese.
- 1 pinch Cayenne pepper
- 2.5ml Made English mustard.

Process
1. Reheat the basic white sauce.
2. Stir in the grated vegetarian cheese, mustard, and cayenne pepper.
3. Reboil and cool.

Sweet and Sour Mushroom Sauce

Yield — 500ml

Process
1. Fry mushrooms in the oil.
2. Add prune quarters, tomato juice, vinegar and seasoning, bring to the boil and simmer in oven gas 4, 180°C for 45 minutes.
3. If the sauce is too thin reduce by boiling and serve.

Ingredients
- 10ml Oil.
- 450g Button mushrooms.
- 120g Dried prunes stoned and cut into quarters.
- 150ml Apple juice.
- 150ml Tomato juice (tomato juice and water).
- 15ml Cider or wine vinegar.
- 2.5ml Thyme.
- Salt and Pepper.

Basic Preparations — Dressings

Dressings

Basic Oil & Vinegar Dressing, Yoghurt Dressing, Vegan Mayonnaise, Cocktail Sauce, Nut creams, Cashewnut & Gooseberry Dressing, Pesto Dressing

Basic Oil & Vinegar Dressing

Ingredients
  3   parts Oil (olive or other vegetable oil).
  1   part vinegar, preferably wine vinegar.
       Salt and freshly ground pepper.

Process
Place all ingredients in a screw top bottle or jar and shake to mix just before use.

A variety of other ingredients may be added to the basic dressing such as: crushed garlic, chopped fresh herbs, dried herbs, French mustard, and vegetables eg. shallots, peppers, celery, raw beetroot.

To make a lighter dressing lemon juice may be substituted for vinegar and sunflower oil for olive oil.

Yoghurt Dressing

Yield — 250ml

Ingredients
  200ml Greek yoghurt.
  50ml   Mayonnaise.

Process
Mix and season.

Basic Preparations — Dressings

Mayonnaise

Yield — 300ml

Ingredients
- 2 Yolks of egg (at room temperature).
- 2g English mustard.
- Pinch Cayenne pepper.
- 30mls White wine vinegar.
- 275ml Cold pressed olive oil (at room temperature).
- Salt and freshly ground white pepper.

Process (by hand and food mixer)
1. Put yolks in a bowl.
2. Add the vinegar and whisk.
3. *Slowly* add the oil, whisking cautiously until used up.

Process (by food processor or liquidiser)
1. Place yolks and dry ingredients in the machine and work for a few seconds.
2. With the machine working slowly add the oil.
3. Finish the process by adding the vinegar.

Mayonnaise Variations
Green Sauce: add blended spinach and parsley.
Tartare Sauce: add chopped parsley, capers and gherkins.
Cocktail Sauce: Add tomato purée, lemon juice and a pinch of cayenne pepper.
Pepper Sauce: add raw liquidised green, yellow or red peppers.

Basic Preparations — Dressings

Vegan Mayonnaise

Yield — 200ml

Ingredients
- 50g Blanched almonds.
- Pinch Cayenne pepper.
- 1tsp Salt.
- 175ml Olive oil.
- 20ml White wine vinegar.
- 70ml Water.

Process
1. Grill or roast the almonds until pale gold in colour, in order to bring out the flavour.
2. Place all ingredients, except the olive oil, in a food processor or liquidiser and work until a smooth paste is reached.
3. With the machine working slowly add the oil until it is all used up.
4. Store in a refrigerator and use as required.

Vegetarian Aspic Jelly

Yield — 500ml

Ingredients
- 500ml Double reduced vegetarian brown stock.
- 7–10g Agar-agar.

Process
1. Dissolve agar-agar flakes in the boiling stock.
2. Cool and use as required.

Nut Cream

Yield — 300ml

Ingredients (1)
- 200g   Nuts: almonds, cashews or hazel.
- 200ml Soya milk.
-        Honey or maple syrup to taste.

Ingredients (2)
- 100g   Nuts: almonds, cashews or hazel.
- 100g   Cream cheese.
- 175ml Milk or water.
-        Honey to taste.

Ingredients (3)
- 100g   Nuts: almonds, cashews or hazel.
- 100g   Soft fruit: peach, mango or raspberry.
- 150ml Water or soya milk.
-        Honey or maple syrup to taste.

Process
1. Blanch the nuts to remove the outer skin.
2. Place the blanched nuts on a baking sheet and grill until the nuts *begin* to turn golden brown. (This will bring out the flavour).
3. Grind the nuts in a food processor or liquidiser.
4. Slowly add the other ingredients and blend to a smooth cream.

Basic Preparations — Dressings

Tahini Cocktail Sauce

Yield — 100ml

Ingredients
- 30ml Light tahini.
- 90ml Cold water.
- 4g   Ground sea salt.
- 15ml Lemon juice.
- 1   clove Crushed garlic.
- 10ml Tomato purée.
-       Pinch ground white pepper.

Process
1. Cream the tahini with cold water.
2. Add salt, pepper and garlic.
3. Add lemon juice.
4. Work to a cream.
5. Finish the process by adding tomato purée; this will give the sauce a pale pink colour.

Cashew Nut & Gooseberry Dressing

Yield — 200ml

Ingredients
- 50g   Cashew Nuts.
- 50g   Gooseberries.
- 150ml Sunflower oil.
-        Sea salt and freshly ground white pepper.
- 50ml   Cold water.
- 5g   Grated fresh horse-radish *with*
- 10ml   *Double cream or* 15ml   Horseradish sauce.

Basic Preparations — Dressings

Process
1. Liquidise the Cashew nuts with the gooseberries, horse-radish and water.
2. Slowly add the oil and seasoning.

Pesto

Yield — 5 litres

Ingredients
- 900ml   Fresh basil or
- 30ml   Dried basil with grape brandy and sprig of chopped parsley.
- 5   Cloves crushed garlic.
- 100ml   Cold pressed olive oil.
- 2g   Sea salt.
- 2g   Freshly ground black pepper.
- 25g   Pine nuts (optional).

Process (using fresh basil)
1. Blend all ingredients in a food processor or liquidiser.
2. Store in sealed containers and use as required.

Process (using dried basil)
1. Marinade the dried basil in brandy for 1 hour.
2. Proceed as for fresh basil.

Pesto Dressing
- 1   part Pesto.
- 1   part Wine vinegar.
- 3   part Olive oil.

Basic Preparations — Batters

Batters
Light Crispy Batter, Pancake Batter, Blini, Croutons

Light Crispy Batter

Yield — 100ml

Ingredients
- 50g   Strong unbleached flour.
- 90ml   Ice cold water.
-        Salt to taste.

Process
Whisk all ingredients to a smooth batter.

Pancake Batter

Yield — 250ml

Ingredients
- 125g   Wholemeal flour.
- 250ml   Cow's milk.
- 2   Eggs.
- 2.5g   Salt.

Process
1. Combine salt and flour.
2. Add beaten egg.
3. Gradually add milk to produce a smooth batter.

Vegan Pancakes
Replace cow's milk with soya milk and eggs with 50g soya flour.

Basic Preparations — Batters

Blini

Yield — 10 portions

Ingredients

- 100g Unbleached strong flour.
- 50g   Buckwheat flour.
- 2   Egg yolks.
- 7g   Fresh yeast.
- 120ml Warm milk.
- 2   Egg whites.

Process
1. Cream the yeast and milk.
2. Beat the egg yolk and mix with the yeast mixture and flour.
3. Add milk to the consistency of double cream.
4. Leave to ferment for 1-2 hours.
5. Beat the egg whites until stiff.
6. Fold the beaten whites into fermenting mixture.
7. Rest for 30 minutes.
8. Fry the pancakes in hot oil using a 5cm. pastry cutter to obtain uniform shape.
9. Split and fill or serve from the pan.

Croutons

Process
1. Cut wholemeal bread into required number of 8mm dices.
2. Shallow fry in clarified butter or sesame oil and season with salt or garlic salt.
3. Drain on kitchen paper to remove surplus grease.

Clarified Butter
1. Melt unsalted butter over a low heat.
2. Carefully remove the clear golden liquid discarding the white whey.

Basic Preparations — Useful Information

Useful Information

Approximate Conversion

25 grams	1 ounce
110 grams	4 ounces
450 grams	1 lb
55 mls	2 fl oz
275 mls	½ pt
570 mls	1 pt
1 Litre	1¾ pts
1 inch	2.5 cm
6 inches	15 cm
1 teaspoon	5 mls
1 dessertspoon	10 mls
1 tablespoon	15 mls
1 cup	300 mls

Oven Temperatures

gas mark
1	140°C	) slow oven
2	150°C	) moderate oven
3	170°C	)
4	180°C	)
5	190°C	) hot oven
6	200°C	)
7	220°C	)
8	230°C	) very hot oven
9	240°C	)

Basic Preparations — Useful Information

To thicken 1 litre of liquid
250g	Bread
300-350g	Potatoes
125g	Shortgrain rice
125g	Lentils
0.25 litres	Basic white sauce
25 litres	Basic stock sauce
50g	Arrowroot
50g	Fecule (potato starch)
50g	Cornflour
500g	Fresh pulse
100g	Flour and 100g fat (roux)

To finish 1 litre of liquid
1.25dl	Cream
1.25dl	Wine
75g	Cheese
2	Egg yolks

	1 Teaspoon	1 Dessertspoon	1 Tablespoon
Sugar	5g	13g	25g
Salt	7g	17g	30g
Herbs	1g	2g	5g
Flour	3g	9g	15g
Tomato Purée	6g	16g	34g

CHAPTER 4
Techniques & Catering Applications

In this chapter the author explains various cookery techniques and how they may be applied to catering operations with special consideration being made to vegetarian catering. The cooking methods used are in general the same as for all types of food preparation, however with vegetarian cookery we will discover that less common methods are more widely used and vice versa. The different use of ingredients will in some cases mean that the chef will have to consider the reaction of the ingredient to the cookery method. This chapter also examines traditional cutting and preparation techniques used in the industry and how they may be applied to give a greater variety of presentation to vegetarian dishes and to assist in the cooking of the foods when quicker methods of cookery are used eg. stir-frying.

The section on menu planning shows the considerations that have to be made when preparing menus suitable for vegetarians, to give a meal which is balanced and attractive to the consumer. An important aspect of menu planning is the nutritional content of any dish or meal and is a prime consideration for many consumers as recent surveys have shown. In this chapter the nutrients found in food are considered, with regard to their sources, functions, contribution to a balanced diet together with any effects that might occur because of deficiencies.

Whilst the techniques covered in this chapter are standard to food preparation when considered domestically, preparing larger quantities in a professional situation will mean that various catering techniques may have to be considered.

Techniques & Applications — Cooking Methods

Cooking Methods

A variety of cooking methods are used in the preparation of vegetarian food; in this section a brief examination of each will be carried out. The methods to be considered are listed below:

Stewing	Steaming
Roasting	Baking
Braising	Grilling
Poaching	Micro-wave
Blanching	Boiling
Sweating	Cooking in Paper, Tinfoil or Glass
Frying, Deep, Shallow or Wok	

Stewing
There are two types of stewing: stewing foods in their own juice and stewing with added liquid.

Foods to be stewed in their own juice should have a high natural liquid content or failing that, have a high moisture food cooked with them. This is in order to stop initial burning before the food has time to cook and produce its own cooking liquid.

The food or foods are placed in an ovenproof container and sealed in with a tight fitting lid. For good all round heat to minimise burning, the container should be placed in a pre-heated oven at a temperature between 110-140°C.

During the cooking green vegetables such as peas will lose their bright green colour but other vegetables such as peppers may hold their colour.

The juice produced during cooking can be used as a sauce to serve with the food, usually reduced to concentrate the flavour and thicken slightly.

Food cooked with added liquid, such as beans, should be pre-soaked to re-constitute them and then slowly cooked in water or stock on top of the stove until cooked. It should be noted that fast cooking will initially toughen the beans and then eventually break them up. Therefore a temperature of 100-110°C should be kept.

Roasting
There are three types of roasting, these are: Oven roasting, Pot roasting and Spit roasting. Of the three only oven roasting is generally suitable for cooking vegetarian foods.

Techniques & Applications — Cooking Methods

Foods to be oven roasted eg. potatoes and parsnips are placed into a shallow heatproof container and coated with oil or butter. The cooking takes place in a pre-heated oven at a temperature of 200-250°C for approximately one quarter of the overall cooking time. The temperature is then reduced to 150-200°C for the remaining cooking time. During the cooking there should be periodic basting of the food with the oil or butter present within the container.

The initial high temperature and the basting has the effect of sealing the outside of the food, thus minimising the loss of liquid and nutrients.

Braising
Braising is a slow method of cooking which combines the flavours of a selection of vegetables, herbs and cooking liquid with the braised food.

Green vegetables such as celery and cabbage are first blanched in boiling salted water to set the colour. Root vegetables are not blanched.

The vegetable to be braised is then placed in an ovenproof dish on a bed of herbs and vegetables. Enough liquid (stock) to cover is added and the dish is then placed into a pre-heated oven at a temperature of 140-150°C until tender. The main braised vegetable is removed and the cooking liquid strained and reduced to form an accompanying sauce.

Poaching
This is a gentle method of moist heat for cooking eggs, fruit and vegetables by direct or indirect immersion in a liquid at a temperature between 65-86°C.

This method can be broken down into three variations:
a) Direct immersion in water or stock.
b) Indirect immersion in water.
c) Cooking in order to thicken.
a) Fruit, vegetables and eggs may be placed in sufficient liquid to just cover them. The temperature of the liquid (stock or water) is held to below 85°C, ie: barely bubbling, until the food is cooked.
b) Egg-based mixtures and vegetable mousses are cooked in moulds or dishes, three quarters immersed in a water bath. The bath with its water and dishes may be placed in an oven in order to ensure all round heat at the correct temperature.
c) Egg-based sauces and mixtures eg: Hollandaise sauce and some sponge mixtures need a base of cooked egg yolk, obtained by whisking in a metal bowl over a water bath at 85°C.

Blanching
A very quick method of moist heat cooking, which is used to set the colour and seal in the nutrients of vegetables.

Small amounts of prepared vegetables are immersed in plenty of fast boiling water. The water is brought back to the boil as quickly as possible. The vegetables are removed and placed in cold water to render them cold as soon as possible.

The immersion in boiling water and then cold water enhances the colour of green vegetables as well as retaining most of the nutrients, therefore this method of cookery, along with steaming, is considered preferable for the cooking of vegetables.

The term blanching is used to describe the method of removing skins from soft fruit and tomatoes, by plunging into boiling liquid and then into cold.

The term is also used to describe the method of half cooking chip potatoes by immersing in deep fat at a temperature of 140°C until they are soft and without colour. They are then finished in oil at a temperature of 165°C.

Sweating
A method of cooking vegetables in a small amount of fat, oil or liquid in order to bring out the vegetables' own natural juices without colouring the vegetable.

This method of cooking is used in the preparation of many dishes where the flavour of the vegetable is required and not its colour eg: sweating onions for a White Stock or White Bean Stew.

Frying
There are three basic methods of frying vegetables, these are as follows:

Deep Frying
Cooking by immersion in oil.

Vegetables, such as potatoes, lend themselves to this method of cooking and some pastry items are specially made to take advantage of this method, eg: doughnuts and fritters.

With foods which are cooked from raw, such as potatoes it is advisable to 'blanch' the food first with an oil temperature of 140°C. This will allow the heat to penetrate and cook the food through. A final crisping can then be given, as needed, by immersion in oil at 190°C.

Vegetable oils are ideal for deep frying due to their high smoke point which is caused by a low percentage of free fatty acids. It is the high percentage of free fatty acids that gives

Techniques & Applications — Cooking Methods

olive oil and animal fat their low smoke point — a factor that contributes to decomposition and the production and emission of off-flavours and a white smoke called Acrolein.

Shallow Frying
Cooking in a shallow wide pan in the minimum of oil or fat to barely coat the bottom of the pan. Two points must be stressed when using this method:
(i) The cooking fat or oil and the pan must be hot before the food is placed in it. Failure to do this will cause the food to sweat and stick to the pan. The correct temperature will seal the food, giving it a golden brown finish that will prevent sticking.
(ii) The amount of fat or oil must be the minimum required to coat the pan. Too much will cause food items such as lentil and potato cakes to absorb fat, resulting in their breakup and a poor, greasy flavour.

The following simple method can be used to remove surplus oil from non-battered or breaded foods. The food is removed from the cooking oil and immersed immediately in fast boiling water for one second. It is then drained and used as required.

Wok
The Wok or Chinese frying-pan is a large hemi-spherical steel pan. Although the method is placed under frying, the Wok can also be used for boiling, stewing and braising.

The most common use of the Wok is for 'stir-frying'.

For this, the Wok is heated on an open gas, so that the flames bathe the outside of the Wok. A small amount of oil is placed in and allowed to smoke before adding the vegetables to be cooked. Vegetables cooked with this method are cut into thin strips or small shapes to facilitate quick cooking.

Two to three minutes in the Wok with constant stirring to prevent burning and give even heat penetration will be sufficient to cook most foods.

Foods cooked with this method will have a distinctive flavour similar to that produced by charcoal grilling.

Very rapid frying can also be undertaken causing the food to explode, eg crispy noodles and some Indian breads. The Chinese for rapid cooking is 'Bao'.

Steaming
Of the four methods of cooking involving moist heat, steaming alone with blanching, is considered to be the best for the retention of nutrients and colour. There are two distinct methods of steaming, 'Without Pressure' and 'Under Pressure'.

Without Pressure
Vegetables, legumes and cereals may be steamed by placing them in a perforated container suspended above a saucepan of boiling liquid or stock. A loose-fitting lid is used to cover the container in order to prevent a build-up of steam pressure.

The normal catering steamer operating at atmospheric pressure can be used to produce the same results.

Under Pressure
High pressure steamers are of two types; the small domestic cooker mounted type and the catering high pressure cabinet. In both cases the food is placed in a perforated container and the lid or door closed. Pressure builds up between 3 and 7 psi making the foods cook very quickly. The following are examples of the time taken to steam certain commodities using this method:
1½ minutes green vegetables,
30 minutes legumes (dried Butter Beans),
25 minutes cereals.

Baking
Baking takes place in an oven and is different from roasting and other methods as the food is cooked without the addition of any liquid fat or oil.

Foods that are baked include: yeast products, vegetables, nut loaves, pastry and confectionary.

The foods are placed in the oven at a temperature ranging from 140-240°C. Heat is transferred to the food by radiation for browning; conduction and convection for cooking.

Grilling
This method involves exposing the food to radiated heat either from above or below.

The traditional charcoal grill and the simulated charcoal grill impart a particular taste to the food. However, this method does not lend itself to vegetarian cooking.

Food cooked using this method such as root vegetables, should be half cooked in boiling salted water before grilling. Other foods such as stuffed vegetables are pre-cooked before browning or gratinating under a grill salamander.

Techniques & Applications — Cooking Methods

Microwave

Microwave cooking, unlike more traditional forms of cooking, relies on friction to generate heat and hence cooking.

The microwaves enter the food and agitate the molecules, in a liquid the molecules have more space to move therefore more agitation takes place and the liquid heats up very quickly. In contrast with a dry solid food there is little space to move resulting in low heat production and slower cooking.

Browning of foods is a problem with this type of cooking as there is no radiated heat as in the case of a grill, but some microwave ovens are fitted with browning devices.

With regard to vegetarian cooking a microwave oven can be used for prime cooking of vegetables and reheating of some precooked dishes.

Boiling

There are two methods of boiling vegetables, 'Cold Water Start' and 'Boiling Water Start'; both of these use moist heat.

Cold Water Start

Hard, woody vegetables such as carrot, turnip and old potatoes are usually cooked with this method. As the water is brought to the boil with the immersed vegetables, juices from the vegetables leak into the water which are then replaced by the water. This has the effect of cooking the inside, but with a loss of watersoluble vitamins and colour. If the vegetables are overcooked, drastic loss of colour and disintegration will take place. This can be used to advantage when the liquid as well as the vegetable are to be used, eg purée soup.

Boiling Water Start

Soft leaf and young vegetables such as spring greens, new potatoes and peas are usually cooked with this method. The vegetables are immersed in water at 100°C which has the effect of sealing the outside of the vegetable thus restricting the loss of watersoluble vitamins and colour. However, a prolonged temperature drop when cold vegetables are placed in the water will cause some loss of vitamins and colour. Therefore at least three times as much water to vegetables should be used in order to minimise temperature drop.

As with the Cold Water Start over-cooking will result in colour loss and eventually breakup of the vegetables.

Techniques & Catering Applications — Cooking Methods

Cooking in Paper, Tin-Foil or Glass
Traditionally very tender portions of food are cooked with these methods.

In a paper bag, 'en papillote' method, tender vegetables such as asparagus or fruits such as bananas are placed in one half of a heart shaped sheet of grease-proof paper.

The food is coated with a sauce, butter or oil and folded as in figure 1. The edges are crimped as in figure 2 and the bag placed on a baking sheet and cooked in the oven for 15-20 minutes at a medium setting.

The whole bag is served so that the customer may receive the full aroma and flavour of the cooking.

The above method can be carried out using tin-foil instead of paper.

Under glass, 'sous clouche', the food is placed on an oven proof glass dish, cooked with sauce, brought to the boil on top of the stove and a glass dome placed over the food so that steam and aroma are trapped. The customer served with the dome will receive the full aroma of the food.

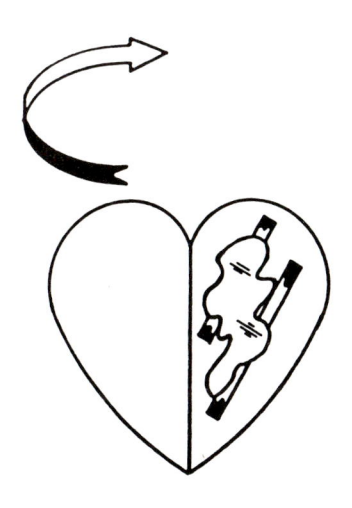

Figure 1

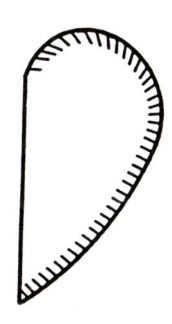

Figure 2

Techniques & Catering Applications — Preparation & Cutting Techniques

Preparation & Cutting Techniques

The traditional preparation of vegetables involves washing and removing all of the skin. In wholefood Vegetarian cooking the vegetables are thoroughly washed and left, where possible, with the skin on. This is in order to preserve the maximum nutritional qualities of the vegetable. However, some vegetables such as swede which have hard and fibrous skins, do require peeling. The peeling of onions and bulb vegetables is also desirable but special care must be exercised as follows:

Do not wash as this will soften the skin.

With a small knife, remove the outer layer and shoot from the top.

Using a small knife, peel the outer skin down to the root.

With a paring action, remove the skin and dirty part of the root, taking great care not to cut into the onion.

Note: If the root is removed, the onion will fall apart when an attempt is made to produce finely chopped onion.

Chopping Vegetables

The method used is as follows:
Hold the vegetable in the left hand with the thumb at the back and the fingers to the front on the cutting area.
Using a large cook's knife at least 10ı long, place the point on the board so as to make like a guillotine with the finger knuckles of the left hand acting as a guide for the blade.
The thumb pushes the vegetable towards the blade.

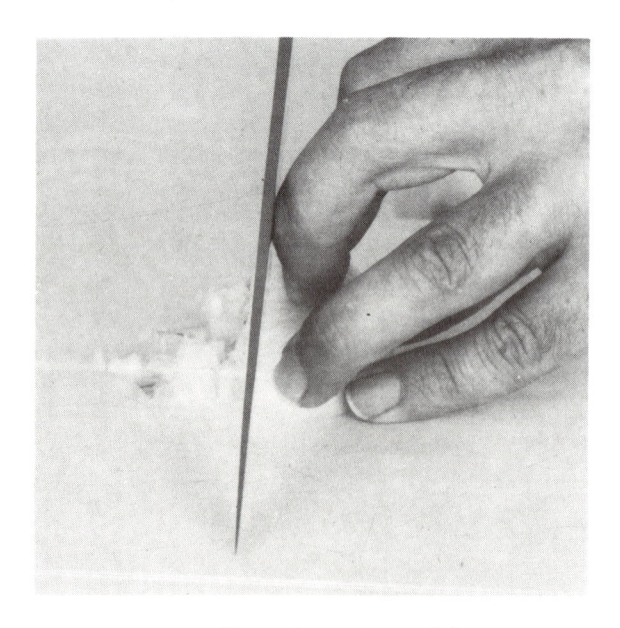

Chopping Vegetables

Techniques & Catering Applications — Preparation & Cutting Techniques

A selection of Chopped Vegetables

Turning Root Vegetables

Vegetables such as potatoes and carrots may be shaped using a small cook's knife (4") into barrel shapes, the method used is as follows:

Hold the vegetable between the thumb and index finger of the left hand. Hold the knife with the right hand so that only 1" of the blade can be used. Start cutting with the right thumb placed over the left hand thumb and the blade near the left hand index finger. Draw the blade in an arc towards the thumbs. Move the vegetable round and repeat.

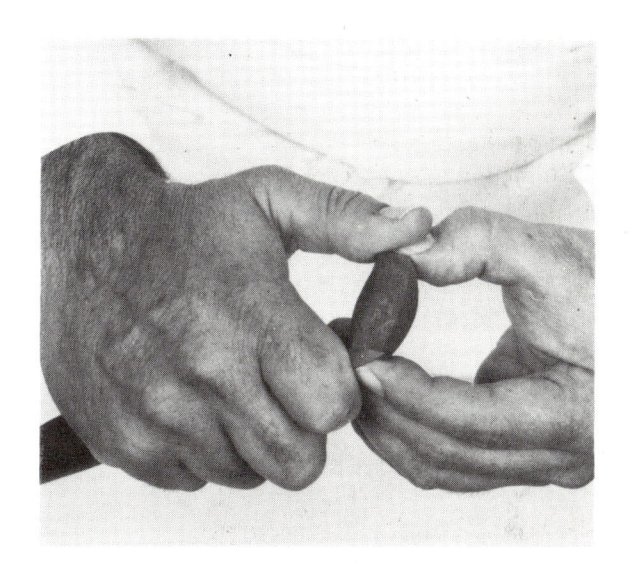

Turning Root Vegetables

A selection of Turned Vegetables

Techniques & Catering Applications — Preparation & Cutting Techniques

Turning Mushrooms

Mushroom caps may be decorated with grooves radiating out from the centre, the method used is as follows:
Hold the dry but clean mushroom in the left hand between the thumb and index finger.
Hold a small cook's knife in the right hand by placing the thumb on top and first two fingers underneath at right angles to the knife on the hilt.
Bring the mushroom to the knife so that the blade rests across the centre and the knuckle of the right hand index finger rests on the mushroom. Move the mushroom away and down in an arc to produce a shallow curved cut from the centre to the outer edge. Move the mushroom round and repeat.
When finished, a star may be placed in the centre using the point of the knife.

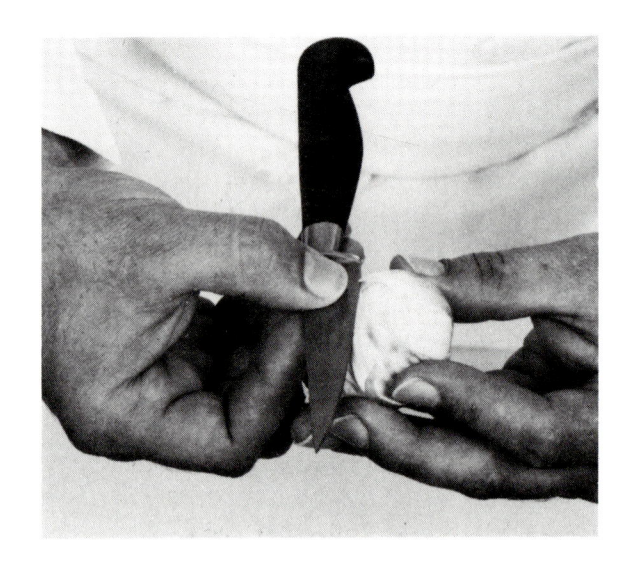

Turning Mushrooms

Stages of Turning Mushrooms

Techniques & Catering Applications — Preparation & Cutting Techniques

Spoon Moulding
Equipment needed
2 spoons of the same size, teaspoons, dessert spoons or tablespoons.
1 bowl of very hot water,
1 tray on which to place the moulded goods.

Process (assuming right-handed person)
Place both spoons in hot water.
Take one spoon in the right hand and scrape it across the mixture to be moulded so as to overfill the spoon.
Take the other spoon in the left hand and remove the mixture from the right hand spoon by using the side of the left hand spoon to cut the mixture out.
Repeat this process from left spoon to right spoon and back, until a smooth three-sided egg shape has been formed.
Place the shape on the tray.
Wash the spoons in hot water and repeat.

Spoon Moulding Stage One

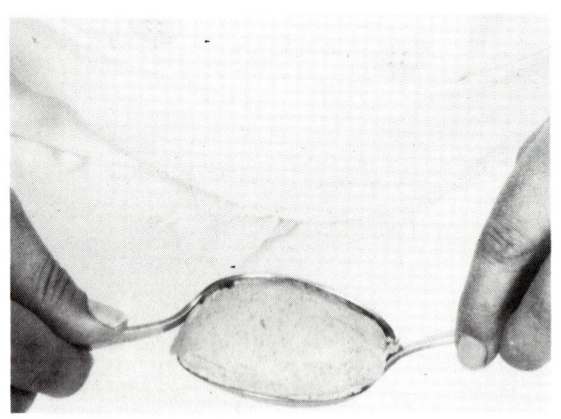

Techniques & Catering Applications — Preparation & Cutting Techniques

Spoon Moulding Stage Two

Spoon Moulding Stage Three

Menu Planning

Many of the traditional concepts of a menu sequence do not apply to vegetarian catering, ie:

    Appetiser
    Soup
    Fish
    Meat
    Sweet
    Savoury

The need to ensure the continuation of creative vegetarian food production would make it wrong to restrict the cuisine to the straight-jacket of a rigid menu format. However in the eyes of the public a menu must have some recognisable form, for this reason, the following guide lines are enclosed.

Starter Course
Light, very appetising food, which may be hot, or cold, liquid or solid, and above all small in amount and very attractive to the eye.

Middle Courses
Dishes should be light, attractively arranged and of moderate portion size.

If there is more than one middle course then the order should be from light and small, finishing with the heaviest dishes.

Finishing Courses
These can be sweet or savoury but care must be exercised to ensure that the foods are not too heavy, bearing in mind that wholefoods are very filling.

Other Considerations when Planning Menus
Season. Two fundamental considerations should be taken when planning menus. Suitability should be in terms of the selection of dishes eg: warming food in winter and refreshing food in summer, and also seasonal availability to ensure that costs are kept low and that foods are served at their best.

Equipment. The primary consideration for the preparation and service of food is whether or not sufficient equipment is available. It is preferable to use several pieces of equipment rather than one.

Staff. Consideration must be given to the skills of the cooking and service staff and whether or not they are sufficient to cope with the dishes on the menu, eg: can the chefs make wholemeal puff pastry or can the waiter cook a flambé dish in the restaurant.

Cost. When considering the cost of a particular menu, attention should be paid toward whether the menu is to run for a period of time or if it is a special 'one off' event; in addition, factors such as seasonal fluctuations and inflation should also be taken into account.

Customer. The menu must be tailored to accommodate customer needs, these may persist over a period of time or may apply for a special event such as a wedding or a business promotion.

Techniques & Catering Applications — Menu Planning

Ingredients. Consideration must be given to nutritional needs and balance when planning menus. Main ingredients should not be used more than once in a menu, eg: it would be wrong to have a mushroom soup followed by a mushroom goulash.

Flavour and Texture. Once again balance is a major consideration in this aspect of menu planning. Particular care should be taken with hot and strong flavoured foods such as curry; these should not be served before light mild foods as the flavour of the latter would not be fully appreciated.

Aesthetic Appeal. The meal as a whole must look appealing to the customers eye with regard to colour balance and texture in that a meal does not look too heavy or light. A balance of cooking methods should also be used so as not to give the impression that the meal is not all 'boiled' or 'fried'.

The following are examples of menus which take account of some of the preceding considerations.

Spring Menu

Avocado Cocktail

★ ★ ★ ★

Egg in Cocotte with Ratatouille

★ ★ ★ ★

Spinach and Green Pepper Fillo Cake
Tabouli Salad — Green salad and Baked Potatoes

★ ★ ★ ★

Fruit Crumble
with
Nut Cream

Techniques & Catering Applications — Menu Planning

Summer Menu

Tomato Mousse

★ ★ ★ ★

Stir Fried Vegetables in a Potato Basket

★ ★ ★ ★

Mushroom Stroganoff with Fresh Green Noodles
A Selection of Salads
Bean
Vegetable
Green

★ ★ ★ ★

Fresh Fruit Salad
or
Fresh Strawberries
with
Cream or Yoghurt

Techniques & Catering Applications — Menu Planning

Autumn Menu

Hot Cheese Mushrooms
with
Tartare Sauce

★ ★ ★ ★

Cream of Leek Soup

★ ★ ★ ★

Fillo Bean Bags with Red Pepper Sauce
Dauphine Potatoes and Green Salad

★ ★ ★ ★

Apple Strudel

Winter Menu

Tempura
with
Tahini Cocktail Sauce

★ ★ ★ ★

Fresh Tomato and Basil Soup

★ ★ ★ ★

Aduki Bean and Mushroom Pudding
Anna Potatoes — Broccoli in a Cheese Sauce

★ ★ ★ ★

Fruit Fool
or
Carob Mousse

Christmas Menu

Spinach Roulade

★ ★ ★ ★

Miso Soup

★ ★ ★ ★

Raised Nut and Vegetable Pie
with
Sweet and Sour Mushroom Sauce
Pot Roast   Red Pepper and Parnsips
Swiss Style Potatoes

★ ★ ★ ★

Vegetarian Christmas Pudding or Raspberry and Peach Wendy

Techniques & Catering Applications — Menu Planning

Cold Buffet Menu

Melon and Blackberry Cocktail
with Ginger Dressing
Tomato Mousse
Hummus with Pitta Bread

★ ★ ★ ★

Raised Nut and Vegetable Pie
Mushroom and Tomato Pizza
Walnut and Green Pepper Roast

★ ★ ★ ★

Selection of Salads
Bean
Pasta
Potato
Green

★ ★ ★ ★

Honey and Almond Custard
Gooseberry and Mango Flan
Fresh Fruit Salad
Nut Cream

Hot Buffet

Egg Rolls — Garlic Mushrooms
Stuffed Eggs Chimay

★ ★ ★ ★

Chick-pea and Pepper Couscous
Vegetable Strudel
Bean Crumble

★ ★ ★ ★

Baked Potatoes   Baker Style Potatoes
Anna Potatoes
Ratatouille   Selection of Salads

★ ★ ★ ★

Pears in Fillo Pastry
Baked Apples
Fresh Fruit Salad

Nutrition

Nutrition is the study of food, the nutrients it contains, their uses to the body and the fate of any waste products. In this section, the nutrients, their sources, functions, effects of a deficiency and contribution to a balanced vegetarian diet are considered.

Nutrients are chemical substances found in food, which when digested, if necessary and absorbed serve some useful purposes in the body, such as; providing energy, materials for growth and repair of substances which regulate body processes. The nutrients found in food are; *carbohydrates, fats, proteins, vitamins, minerals* and *water*. Dietary fibre or roughage is not considered to be a nutrient as it is not absorbed by the body, but as it does serve a useful purpose many believe the definition should be altered to include it.

Table to show Nutrient function

Nutrients Providing Energy	Nutrients Providing Growth and Repair	Regulatory Substances
Carbohydrates	Proteins	Minerals
Fats	Minerals	Vitamins
Proteins	Water	Water
	Some fats	(Proteins)

Carbohydrates

The function of carbohydrates in the body is to provide energy. Excess carbohydrate in our diet is converted into body fat. Dietary carbohydrates are divided into two groups, the sugars which include glucose, fructose, sucrose and lactose, and starches or the non-sugars.

Over consumption of refined sugar (sucrose) and its products, such as cakes, biscuits, ice-cream and 'sweets' has led to an increase in tooth decay in many 'westernised' countries and has been linked with an increase in the occurrence of diseases such as heart disease, diabetes, colon cancer and obesity, known collectively as the diseases of affluence. It is therefore now recommended that our refined sugar intake is drastically reduced and that natural sugars and starches should provide the carbohydrate intake in our diet.

Sources: Natural Sugars: Honey, fruits (especially dried), young root vegetables like carrots, milk (as lactose). Starch: Wheat and other grains, pasta, potatoes, oatmeal, wholemeal bread and flour.

Techniques & Catering Applications — Nutrition

Fats

Fats have a number of functions in the body; they provide an energy source and store, protect vital organs like the heart, liver and kidneys, provide a source of the essential fatty acids like linoleic acid needed for tissue growth and repair and must be provided by the diet and provide a source of the fat soluble vitamins A, D, E and K. They also provide an important contribution to the texture and palatability of foods.

Saturated Fats are naturally solid at room temperature, large quantities are found in animal fats.

Chemical structure:

$$H-\underset{H}{\overset{H}{C}}-\underset{H}{\overset{H}{C}}-\underset{H}{\overset{H}{C}}-\underset{H}{\overset{H}{C}}-\underset{H}{\overset{H}{C}}-H$$

C = Carbon
H = Hydrogen
— = Chemical bond

Each carbon has its full complement of hydrogen atoms.

Unsaturated Fats are naturally liquid at room temperature, large quantities are found in vegetable fats/oils.

Chemical structure:

$$H-\underset{H}{\overset{H}{C}}-\underset{H}{\overset{H}{C}}=\overset{H}{C}-\underset{H}{\overset{H}{C}}-\underset{H}{\overset{H}{C}}-H$$

= Double bond

The second and third carbon do not have a full complement of hydrogen atoms, so form a double bond with each other. In mono-unsaturated fats there is one double bond and in poly-unsaturated fats many double bonds.

Over consumption of fatty foods, especially those containing high levels of saturated fats, has also been associated with the increased occurrence of the disease of affluence.

Recommendations are now, that the fat content of our diet should be reduced as a whole and particularly the saturated fat content. A vegetarian diet would usually meet these recommendations, if high quantities of dairy products and eggs are not consumed. Corn oil, safflower oil, soya bean and sunflower oil have high unsaturated fat content.

Proteins

Proteins are required by the body for growth and repair and for the formation of some hormones, antibodies and enzymes which are essential for controlling the chemical reactions within our bodies. Proteins can also be used to provide energy.

Proteins are composed of long chains of Amino Acid Units. Twenty amino acids occur commonly in foods and the human body. Of these twenty, eight are essential for adults and nine for children. These essential amino acids must be provided by the diet as they cannot be made in the body or not in sufficient quantity, like the non-essential ones.

The use any particular protein has to the body (known as protein quality) is determined by the level of the limiting essential amino acid within it, which is the essential amino acid most deficient in the protein, for example, Lysine is the limiting amino acid in grains and methionine in legumes. Grains however have a high methionine content and legumes a high lysine content, if the two are eaten together, for example by eating beans on toast, they will complement each other; that is, the deficiency of lysine in the grain is made up by the high level in the legumes and vice versa with methionine. Thus by eating two protein foods which complement each other, together, protein quality is increased. In a vegetarian diet this can be achieved by eating the following combinations: milk products and grains (bread and cheese or millet pudding); grains and beans, peas, lentils (beans and pasta or rice and lentils or beans); beans, peas and lentils with nuts and seeds (hummus). Good sources of protein are: whole grains, wholemeal bread and flour, soya flour, peanuts, walnuts, hazelnuts, beans, pulses, lentils and peas, dairy products, and eggs.

A protein deficiency is unlikely but care should be taken that suffucient energy giving foods in the form of carbohydrates and fats are consumed, or protein will be used to provide energy, rather than for its more vital roles such as growth and repair.

Vitamins
Vitamins are divided into two groups, fat soluble, dissolving in fats/oils but not in water and water soluble dissolving in water but not in fats/oils.

Fat Soluble Vitamins
1. Vitamin A — Retinol
   Necessary for the formation of visual purple, needed for proper vision in dim light, for healthy skin and healthy mucus membranes, such as those lining the respiratory tract.
   A deficiency results in poor vision in dim light, poor skin and lowered resistance to infection and ultimately results in incurable eye disorders or blindness.
   Sources: Retinol itself is only found in animal products including dairy products, and is added to margarine. Carotene, an orange/red pigment found in fruits and vegetables is converted to vitamin A in the body. Good sources of carotene are

carrots, tomatoes, dark green vegetables including spinach, watercress, broccoli and apricots. An excessive intake is unlikely to occur with a normal diet but illness (hypervitaminosis) has resulted after large quantities of vitamin pills have been taken.

2. *Vitamin D — Cholecalciferol*
Necessary for the proper absorption and laying down of calcium and phosphorus to form bones and teeth. A deficiency results in rickets in children, characterised by bow legs and knock-knees and osteomalacia in adults where the bones become soft, weak and painful.

Sources: Vitamin D itself is only found in animal foods including dairy products and eggs and like vitamin A is added to margarine. The major source for most people is through the action of sunlight on the skin, which converts any fatty components there to vitamin D. An excessive intake of vitamin D is harmful, resulting in calcium being deposited in the soft tissues of the body.

3. *Vitamin E — The Tocopherols*
A natural antioxidant (prevents oxidation and is added to vegetable oils to prevent the oxidation of unsaturated fats which causes rancidity) whose functions are thought to be related to this. It is also thought to be involved in wound healing and cell functioning and formation. Research is still being carried out to discover its precise functions and the effects of a deficiency.

Sources are wheat germ, vegetable oils, especially cold pressed oils, milk, eggs and nuts.

4. *Vitamin K*
Necessary for the formation of Prothrombin, which clots the blood.

A deficiency is unlikely because of the intestinal bacteria which make it, although it is thought that these are affected by antibiotics. A deficiency would cause haemorrhaging, bruising and the failure of wounds to stop bleeding.

Sources: Found in a wide range of foods including green vegetables, cereals and sea vegetables. It is synthesised by bacteria in the intestine.

Water Soluble Vitamins

1. *Vitamin B^1 Thiamine*
    Involved in the oxidation of carbohydrates to release energy in respiration.
    A deficiency results in beri-beri, where muscular weakness occurs, the nerves break down and the heart beat is irregular. In dry beri-beri the patient suffers from tissue wastage and in wet beri-beri, oedema, which is fluid in the tissues.
    Sources: Whole cereals, cereal germ and bran, potatoes, peas, beans, nuts and milk. Brewers yeast and yeast extracts are also good sources of this and other B vitamins but as they are eaten in such small quantities they do not make an important contribution to the diet. Thiamine is easily lost during cooking and storage.

2. *Vitamin B^2 Riboflavin*
    Like Thiamine, Riboflavin is involved in obtaining energy from carbohydrates.
    A deficiency results in sore or cracked lips, a red and swollen tongue and eye irritability. Symptoms which may result from a lack of the other B vitamins as well. A diet deficient in Riboflavin will usually be deficient in other nutrients as well.
    Sources: Cheese, eggs, milk, potatoes, mushrooms, vegetables, cereals, almonds. Easily destroyed, especially by light.

3. *Vitamin B^3 Nicotinic Acid (Niacin)*
    Like Thiamine and Riboflavin, Nicotinic acid is also involved in obtaining energy from carbohydrates.
    A deficiency results in Pellagra or the disease of the three Ds as its symptoms are dementia (mental disorders), diarrhoea and dermatitis (skin disorders).
    Sources: Is widely distributed in plant foods, the main sources are bran, peanuts, wheatgerm, wholewheat flour, mushrooms, vegetables and pluses.

4. *Vitamin B^6 Pyridoxine*
    Functions in the enzyme system concerned with protein synthesis.
    Deficiency is rare, but can result in anaemia, depression and nervous disorders.
    Sources: Wheatgerm, bran, peanuts, hazelnuts, cereals and pulses. Destroyed by heat and light.

Techniques & Catering Applications — Nutrition

5. *Folic Acid — Folate*
   Needed for the proper formation of blood cells.
   Deficiency causes anaemia, exhaustion and depression, and has occurred during pregnancy and in elderly people.
   Sources: Wheatgerm, bran, whole grains, vegetables including spinach, parsley, broccoli and watercress. Large amounts are lost during cooking.

6. *Vitamin B^{12} Cobalamin (Cyanocobalamine)*
   Necessary for growth and red blood cell formation, it is a complex vitamin containing the element Cobalt.
   A deficiency causes pernicious anaemia, which is almost always caused by a failure to absorb the vitamin rather than a dietary deficiency. Vegans are the only people in whom a dietary deficiency has been observed. A dietary supplement of cobalamin should therefore be taken by vegans.
   Sources: Found only in foods of animal origin, including milk, milk products and eggs. Traces are found in sea vegetables, yeast extracts, miso and shoyu, but because of the small quantities these foods are eaten in they do not make a significant contribution to the diet.

7. *Vitamin C Ascorbic Acid*
   Needed for the formation of body tissues, especially connective tissue or collagen which supports, separates and protects the other tissues and organs of the body, and the proper healing of wounds. It aids the absorption of iron in the intestine.
   A deficiency causes sore and bleeding gums, the failure of wounds and bones to heal properly, bruising and anaemia, finally resulting in scurvy and death. Some of these symptoms have been shown by people who have been taking excessive quantities of vitamin C and then reduced their intake drastically.
   Sources: Found in all fruits and vegetables, particularly good sources are blackcurrants, citrus fruits, soft summer fruits like strawberries, gooseberries and raspberries, red and green peppers, brussel sprouts, cauliflower, spinach and cabbage. It is not found in pulses and cereals. Least stable of all the vitamins, destroyed by heat and when cut surfaces are exposed to air.

Mineral Elements (Salts)

Some mineral elements are present and therefore required by the body in relatively large amounts, for example, Calcium, Iron, Phosphorus, Sodium and Chlorine. These are termed the major mineral elements. Others, like Cobalt, Copper, Fluorine and Iodine are present and therefore required in relatively small amounts, these are known as trace elements. Excessive intakes of mineral elements can prove harmful.

Of all the major mineral elements and trace elements, three require special consideration in the vegetarian diet (as in all British diets) — Calcium, Iron and Iodine.

Calcium

Needed for the proper formation of bones and teeth, for blood clotting and for proper functioning of muscles and nerves.

Deficiency results in irritability, nervour disorders and stunted growth and rickets in children.

Sources: cheese, skimmed milk, yoghurt, soya beans and flour, almonds, brazil and hazelnuts, sunflower and sesame seeds.

Iron

Needed for the proper formation of haemoglobin, the red pigment in blood which carries oxygen around the body. A deficiency causes anaemia, resulting in lethargy, a lack of energy, dizziness and headaches.

Sources: dried fruit, especially peaches and apricots, dates, figs, prunes and prune juice, pulses, molasses, wholemeal flour and bread, whole cereal, and egg yolk.

Its absorption is greatly aided by the presence of vitamin C, a breakfast therefore including a whole cereal, wholemeal toast, orange juice and possibly an egg, will have a high usuable iron content.

Iodine

Needed for the formation of the hormone thyroxine, in the thyroid gland.

Deficiency causes a goitre, sometimes called Derbyshire neck, a swelling of the thyroid gland.

Sources: sea vegetables, vegetables grown near the sea or if iodine is present in the soil, sea salt and iodized table salt.

Water
Essential to life, providing a medium in which chemical reactions can take place and chemical substances such as enzymes and nutrients can be dispersed and a means of transport for nutrients in the blood and waste products in urine.

Deficiency: humans can survive for only a few days without water in one form or another, after which death results. Water cannot be stored in the body so regular intake is essential.

Sources: all foods and beverages, the latter being at least 85% water. Fresh vegetables and fruits have a high water content.

Dietary Fibre
Speeds up the passage of food through the digestive system, preventing constipation and possibly other more serious conditions, such as colon cancer, diverticulosis and hiatus hernia.

Sources: wholemeal flour and bread, whole cereals, bran, pulses, vegetables and fruits especially dried fruits such as apricots, prunes and peaches.

Balanced Diets
In a vegetarian diet, as in any other, it is important that it is properly balanced, that is the correct amounts of nutrients are taken into the body. Providing that adequate amounts of a variety of different foods, like fresh vegetables, fruits (dried and fresh), pulses, grains, nuts, seeds and some dairy products are consumed daily, this should be achieved, with Vegans usually requiring a Vitamin B^{12} (cobalamine) supplement as they do not consume dairy products.

Particular care should be taken when planning vegan diets for young children and pregnant or lactating women, if a properly balanced diet is to be provided, with the latter normally requiring supplements of Vitamin D and calcium, as calcium gluconate, as well as Vitamin B^{12}.

Suggested Complements
Most recipes are followed by a suggested complement which may help in producing a well balanced menu.

Commodity Purchase Sizes

Sugars
Granulated	1kg, 50 kg.
Caster	1 kg, 2 kg, 3 kg, 25 kg.
Icing	500 gr, 1 kg, 3 kg.
Demerara	500 gr, 3 kg.
Dark Moist	500 gr, 3 kg, 50 kg.
Light Soft	500 gr, 3 kg, 50 kg.
Fondant	12.5 kg.
Golden Syrup	500 gr, 1 kg, 7.26 kg.
Black Treacle	500 gr, 1 kg, 7.26 kg.
Honey (pure)	500 gr, 1 kg, 3.5 kg.

Flour
Strong	1.5 kg, 32 kg (McDougalls Plain & SR — 3 kg, 12.5 kg).
Soft	1.5 kg, 32 kg.
Wholemeal 100%	1.5 kg, 32 kg.
Brown Flour (Wheatmeal) 85%	1.5 kg, 32 kg.
Rye Flour	32 kg.

Dried Fruits
Currants	500 gr, 3 kg, 12.5 kg, 15 kg.
Sultanas	500 gr, 3 kg, 12.5 kg, 15 kg.
Raisins	500 gr, 3 kg, 12.5 kg.
Mixed Peel	500 gr, 12.5 kg.
Cherries, whole	500 gr, 12.5 kg.
Cherries, whole and broken	5 kg.
Dates	3 kg.
Prunes	3 kg.
Mixed Fruit (Sultanas, Currants (Peel)	2 kg.

Techniques & Catering Applications — Commodity Purchase Sizes

Jams

Raspberry)	
Strawberry)	3 lbs, 7 lbs, 12.5 kg.
Blackcurrant)	
Mixed Fruit)	
Mincemeat	3 lbs, 7 lbs, 12.5 kg.
Mincemeat Raw Sugar	12.5 kg.

Nuts

Almonds, split	1 kg, 5 kg, 12.5 kg.
Almonds, nib	1 kg, 5 kg, 12.5 kg.
Almonds, ground	1 kg, 5 kg, 12.5 kg.
Almonds, strip	1 kg, 5 kg, 12.5 kg.
Almonds, whole	1 kg, 5 kg, 12.5 kg.
Almonds, flaked	1 kg, 5 kg, 12.5 kg.
Walnuts, whole	1 kg, 5 kg.
Walnuts, whole and broken	1 kg, 5 kg.
Hazels, whole	1 kg, 5 kg.
Hazels, ground	1 kg, 3 kg, 5 kg, 12.5 kg.
Peanuts, flaked	5 kg, 12.5 kg.

Fruit

Oranges	Box of varying counts, common sizes are '88' and '112' referring to number in a box.
Apples	Boxes of varying weights and sizes. English: 20, 22, 30 lb.
Bananas	Box — usual sizes 28 lb and 40 lb. Note: a bunch of some 6-8 bananas is referred to as a 'Hand'.
Lemon	Boxed various counts but usual at this time 100-130.
Grapefruit	Boxed — counts vary but usual is 48-large, 56-medium, 64-small.
Pear	Boxed various sizes and counts.
Melon	Open trays of 10 kg — counts vary; 6 per tray (large) to 14 per tray (small).

Techniques & Catering Applications — Commodity Purchase Sizes

Vegetables

Potatoes	'Bag' standard size 25 kg (55.1 lb).
Cabbage	'Net' Green bag. Various sizes but most common is 28 lb. Types — Savoy — green, open heart. — Primo — firm heart. — Dutch white — usual for salad.
Carrots	'Bag' — paper bags usual size 12½ kg.
Onions	'Bag' — coloured net usual size 25 kg.
Swede	'Net' — purple net usual size 28 lb.
Beetroot	'Net' — dark purple net usual size 28 lb.
Cauliflower	'Crate dozen', dependent on size, usually 12 in wooden crate.
Lettuce	'Box' packed in 12's.
Cucumber	'Box' size 12-18 ie: size represents count per box. Class II are usually bent and mis-shaped.
Tomatoes	'Chip', cardboard box — English are 12 lb. Continental sometimes 13 lb and in a wooden tray.
Mustard and Cress	'Tray', usually polystryene tray of 16 punnets, referred to in the trade as Hot and Cold.
Mushroom	'Chip' — button mushroom in baskets of 4 lb. but 'open' mushroom usually in baskets of 3 lb
Spring Onion	'Dozen', usually bundles of 12 — ½ oz bunches.
Peppers	All colours — common sizes 6 lb. and 8 lb. boxes
Celery	'Box', usually in boxes of 12. 'Heads' which refers to 1 plant.
Parsley	'Boat' — wooden box usually of 5 lb. weight.
Leeks	Open crate — usually 14 lb per tray.
Parsnips	'Net' — usually a white net container 28 lb.

Canned Fruit

A 5	822 gr.
A 10 or K C 3	2.65 kg.

Techniques & Catering Applications — Commodity Purchase Sizes

Chocolate
Chocolate, dark	3 kg.
Chocolate, light	3 kg.
Chocolate, couveture	5 kg, 50 kg.
Chocolate, blended kibbled	12.5 kg.

Spices
Pepper, white	600 gr, 3.5 kg.
Pepper, black	600 gr, 3.5 kg.
Pepper, whole black	1 lb.
Pepper, whole white	18 oz.
Mixed Spice	12 oz, 500 gr, 2.5 kg.
Ginger	12 oz, 500 gr, 2.5 kg.
Cinnamon	12 oz, 500 gr, 2.5 kg.
Paprika	550 gr, 1 kg.
Curry Powder	600 gr, 1 kg.
Nutmeg, ground	500 gr, 2.5 kg.
Nutmeg, whole	500 gr.
Chilli Powder	12 oz, 500 gr.
Mixed Herbs	3.25 oz, 500 gr.
Oregano	3 oz, 500 gr.
Bay Leaves	3 oz, 500 gr, 1 kg.
Sage	4.5 oz, 500 gr.
Caraway Seeds	500 gr.
Cloves, whole	10 oz.
Mint	180 gr.
Parsley	130 gr.
Breadcrumbs	2.5 kg.
Salt	3 kg, 25 kg.

CHAPTER 5
Processes & Recipes Starting Courses

The processes and recipes shown in this chapter are those most suitable for starting courses, they may be used for snacks or main courses by increasing the portion size according to the needs of any particular catering operation. The different processes contained in the chapter are indexed below in three broad categories as shown.

Cocktails, Patés, Dips, Mousses & Vegetable Dishes
Fruit Cocktails
Patés
Vegetable Cocktails
Vegetable Dips & Tempura
Hot Stuffed Mushrooms
Vegetable Mousses
Soups
Cold Soups
Cream & Veloute Soups
Clear Soups
Purée Soups
Whole Vegetable & Pulse Soups
Egg & Souffle Dishes
Roulade
Souffle
Scrambled Egg
Eggs in Cocotte
Poached Eggs
Stuffed Hard Boiled Eggs
Omelets
Savoury Flans

Processes & Recipes — Starting Courses

Cocktails, Patés, Dips, Mousses & Vegetable Dishes

Fruit Cocktail

Yield — 5 covers

Process
1. Use Paris goblets or sundae dishes.
2. Arrange the fruit in the container with a small amount of sauce or juice and a contrasting garnish.
3. Do not overfill the container.

Fruits and dressings that may be used

6	Oranges or grapefruits.
1	Melon (Honeydew)
6	Peaches.
7	Apricots
5	Poached pears
25g	Honey for citrus fruit.
50ml	Yoghurt dressing (see basic preparation) for peaches, apricots or pears or use a spiced dressing.
5g	Diced preserved root ginger for melon.
5	Blanched mint leaves.

Suggested Complement
Follow by a good protein balance of bean and grain or dairy products.

Processes & Recipes — Starting Courses

Paté

Yield — 5 portions

Process
1. (a) Using pulses: soak and cook, save the cooking liquid.
   (b) Using vegetables: very finely chop and sweat in own juice until soft.
2. Place in a food processor with other flavouring agents and work to a paste.
3. Add enough vegetable stock or cooking liquid to produce a soft but not liquid paste.
4. Season to taste.

Hummus
- 225g Chick peas.
- 70ml Tahini.
- 30ml Lemon juice.
- 50ml Olive oil.
- 2 Cloves crushed garlic.
- Salt and pepper to taste.

Variation: Add 5ml powdered cumin.

Suggested Complement
A generally well balanced dish, but can be served with wholemeal bread or pitta bread.

Mushroom and Lentil Paté
- 225g Whole lentils, green or brown.
- 225g Mushrooms.
- 30ml Olive oil.
- Black pepper and sea salt to taste.

Variation: Replace the lentils with any of the beans.

Processes & Recipes — Starting Courses

Nut & Mushroom Paté
- 500g   Mushrooms.
- 50g   Finely chopped onions
- 250g   Finely chopped nuts (walnuts, hazelnuts).
- 50g   Wholemeal breadcrumbs

       Sea salt and freshly ground black pepper to taste.

Suggested Complement
Serve with wholemeal bread or grain dish.

Vegetable Cocktail

Yield 5 portions

Process
1. Wash, dry and shred a lettuce into fine strips.
2. Three-quarters fill containers with the shredded lettuce.
3. Top with prepared vegetable.
4. Just before serving coat with mayonnaise or tahini cocktail sauce.
5. Garnish with lemon and watercress.

Avocado Cocktail
- 3   Ripe avocado pears peeled and diced.
- 300ml   Cocktail sauce.
- 1   Lemon sliced.

Mushroom and Pasta Shell Cocktail
- 300ml   Tahini cocktail sauce.
- 1   Lemon sliced.
- 150g   Quartered mushrooms.
- 50g   Cooked wholewheat or green pasta shells.

Processes & Recipes — Starting Courses

Vegetable Dips & Tempura

Yield 5 portions

Process
1. Wash and, if necessary, peel the vegetables.
2. (a) For raw dip, cut vegetables into fine strips, rounds, florets or shapes.
   (b) For tempura, prepare vegetables as for the raw dip and coat in flour and a light batter (see basic preparation).
3. Deep-fry battered vegetables in hot oil at 190°C until golden brown.
4. Arrange cooked or raw vegetables around the bowl of dip, eg. garlic mayonnaise, tahini cocktail sauce.

Examples of vegetables for dips and tempura
Cauliflower florets, broccoli heads, carrots, mushrooms, blanched mange-tout, blanched french beans, steamed okra, fresh ginger, pumpkin, persimmon, water chestnuts.

Hot Stuffed Mushrooms

Yield — 5 portions

Process
1. Wash and remove the stalks from the mushrooms.
2. Place the filling on the dark side of one mushroom.
3. Cover with another mushroom and squeeze to form a ball.
4. Pass through seasoned unbleached flour, beaten egg and breadcrumbs, twice.
5. Deep fry in hot oil at a temperature of 180°C until golden brown.
6. Serve with a sauce, garnish with parsley or watercress.

Photograph on Page 133

Processes & Recipes — Starting Courses

Garlic Mushrooms
10	Medium-sized mushrooms.	
2	Cloves garlic peeled and puréed.	)
50g	Butter.	)
10ml	Chopped parsley.	) mixed to a paste
	Freshly ground black pepper.	)
250ml	Tomato sauce (see basic preparations).	

Cheese Mushrooms
10	Medium-sized mushrooms.	
¼	Clove garlic peeled and puréed.	)
50g	Grated vegetarian cheddar cheese.	)
10g	Butter.	) mixed to a paste
	Freshly ground black pepper.	)
250ml	Tartare sauce (see basic preparations).	

Vegetable Mousse

Yield — 5 portions

Process
1. Wash, peel or blanch, if necessary, the main vegetable.
2. Cook the main prepared vegetable and liquidise.
3. Add the other flavour ingredients, wine, seasoning, tomato puree etc.
4. Dissolve the agar agar in a small amount of boiling water.
5. Gently cook the main mixture for 5-10 mins.
6. Add the dissolved agar agar to the mixture.
7. Cool over ice, stirring to aid an even setting.
8. Half-whip the double cream or silken tofu.
9. Fold cream or tofu into the setting mixture.
10. Correct seasoning.
11. Set in a prepared mould or spoon mould.

Processes & Recipes — Starting Courses

Tomato Mousse
- 200g   Whole tomatoes.
- 1   Chopped leaf of basil or pinch of dried basil.
- 15ml   White wine.
- 10g   Agar agar.
- 15ml   Tomato puree.
- 150ml   Silken tofu or Greek yoghurt or double cream.
- Sea Salt, freshly ground black pepper.

Vegetable Mousse
- 250g   Main vegetable (spinach, asparagus, beetroot).
- 7–10g   Agar agar.
- 150ml   Silken tofu or Greek yoghurt or double cream.
- 15ml   White wine or other wine.
- Sea salt, freshly ground black pepper.

Suggested Complement
Serve vegan ie. tofu-based, mousses with wholemeal bread. Cream-based mousses should be served with wholemeal bread and either nuts or other whole dairy produce, not just milk fat, ie. cream or butter.

Soups

Cold Soups

Yield — 5 portions

Process
1. Peel, if necessary and wash all vegetables.
2. Cut all vegetables into a small dice.
3. Liquidise all vegetables with water and bread.
4. Add olive oil slowly.
5. Serve chilled.

Processes & Recipes — Starting Courses

Gazpacho
- 500g   Diced tomato.
- 400g   Diced cucumber.
- 40g   Diced onion.
- 1   Clove garlic, crushed.
- 50g   Fresh soft wholemeal breadcrumbs.
- 25g   Diced red pepper.
- 25g   Diced green pepper.
- 0.5l   Cold water.
- 15ml   Red wine vinegar.
- 200ml   Olive oil.
-         Sea salt and freshly ground black pepper.

Cold Cooked Soups
Cold vegetable or pulse soups may be liquidised with iced water and finished with cream or yoghurt.

Cream and Veloute Soups

Yield — 5 portions

Process
1. Wash and if necessary peel the vegetables.
2. Save one eighth of the main vegetable for the garnish.
3. Cut the remaining vegetables into small dice or slice.
4. Sweat the cut vegetables in butter or oil.
5. Add the liquid and seasoning and three-quarters cook the vegetables.
6. If used, add basic white sauce or basic white stock sauce.
7. Bring to the boil and simmer until cooked.
8. Cut the garnish vegetables into neat 2mm dice and cook in a small amount of stock or water.
9. Remove the seasoning from the soup and liquidise.
10. Reboil and correct consistency by reduction or adding liquid.
11. Add cream or yoghurt or yolk of egg and cream or soya milk.
12. Correct seasoning.
13. Add garnish.

Processes & Recipes — Starting Courses

Cream of Mushroom

375g	Mushrooms.
115g	Finely chopped shallot.
½	Clove of garlic.
5ml	Olive oil.
1l	White vegetable stock.
30ml	Double cream.
15ml	Greek yoghurt.
	Sea salt and freshly ground pepper to taste.

Cream of Vegetable

375g	Fresh single or mixed vegetables.
0.5l	Basic white sauce using milk.
1.25l	Milk.
15g	Finely chopped shallot.
5ml	Sunflower oil or
5g	Butter.
30ml	Double cream (optional).
	Sprig of thyme and parsley.
½	Bayleaf.
	Sea salt and freshly ground pepper to taste.

Suggested Complement
If the soups are made with whole milk or whole milk products eg. yoghurt, the soup is reasonably well balanced. However, if soya milk is used bread, or grain-based dishes should be eaten as an accompaniment.
Note: If soya milk is used to replace cow's milk, boiling will split the soup.

Processes & Recipes — Starting Courses

Veloute of Vegetable

375g	Fresh single or mixed vegetables.
0.5l	Basic white stock sauce.
1.25l	Basic white stock.
15g	Finely chopped shallot.
5ml	Sunflower oil or
5g	Butter.
	Sprig of thyme and parsley.
½	Bayleaf.
30ml	Double cream.
1	Egg yolk.
	Sea salt and freshly ground white pepper to taste.

Clear Soups

Yield — 5 portions

Process
1. Wash and, if necessary, peel the vegetables.
2. Cut the vegetables into small dice.
3. If Miso is used, mix diced vegetables and Miso.
4. Three-quarters whisk egg whites.
5. Mix the egg whites with the vegetables.
6. Add cold stock, herbs and seasoning.
7. Heat to boiling point and simmer for three-quarters of an hour.
8. Strain through a fine cloth.
9. Correct seasoning.
10. Add blanched or cooked garnish.

Processes & Recipes — Starting Courses

Miso Soup
- 25g Leek.
- 25g Celery.
- 25g Carrot.
- 15g Onion.
- 1.75l Double reduced brown vegetable stock.
- 15ml Shoyu.
- 10ml Miso.
- 5g Peeled and finely shredded root ginger.
- 1 Large egg white.
      Sea salt and freshly ground pepper.

Garnish
- 5 Sprigs water cress.
- 50g 1cm cubed regular tofu.

Photograph on Page 132

Clear Vegetable Soup
- 25g Leek.
- 25g Celery.
- 25g Carrot.
- 15g Fennel.
- 15g Shoyu.
- 1.75l Double reduced brown vegetable stock.
- 1 Large egg white.
      Sprig thyme
      Sea salt and freshly ground pepper.

Suggested Complement
Serve with cheese and grain produce.

Processes & Recipes — Starting Courses

Puree Soups — Pulses

Yield — 5 portions

Process
1. Prepare the pulses (see preparation and cooking pulses).
2. Place washed and soaked pulse in a thick bottomed sauce pan and cover with cold vegetable stock or water.
3. Bring to the boil (minimum 10 minutes) and skim
4. Add all other ingredients except salt (salt will toughen the pulse and prolong cooking times).
5. Skim as necessary and simmer until tender.
6. Approximate cooking times:
    Lentils, whole: 45-50 mins.
    Lentils, split: 30-40 mins.
    Beans, whole: 50-100 mins depending on size.
    Peas, whole: 70-100 mins.
    Peas, split: 45-50 mins.
7. Remove seasoning and other ingredients.
8. Liquidise.
9. Season with salt.
10. Reboil, skim as necessary.
11. Serve with croutons (see basic preparations).

Lentil Soup

250g	Lentils — green or red.
60g	Whole onion.
60g	Whole carrot.
1.75l	White vegetable stock.
15ml	Tomato puree (red lentils only).
	Seasoning
	Sprig thyme and parsley.
	Sea salt and freshly ground pepper.
½	Bay leaf.

Processes & Recipes — Starting Courses

White Bean Soup
- 250g — Beans — Haricot or Blackeye or Butter or mixed.
- 30g — Whole onion.
- 60g — Whole carrot.
- 30g — Celery stick.
- 15g — Fennel.
- 30g — Leek.
- 1.75l — White vegetable stock.
  Seasoning
  Sprig thyme, parsley and chervil.
- ½ — Bay leaf.
  Sea salt and freshly ground pepper to taste.

Kidney Bean Soup
- 250g — Beans — red or black or pinto or mixed.
- 30g — Whole onion.
- 30g — Celery.
- 15g — Fennel.
- 1.5l — Brown vegetable stock.
- 0.25l — Red wine.
  Seasoning
  Sprig thyme, parsley and chervil.
  Sea salt and freshly ground pepper.

Suggested Complement
As a general rule most pulse soups should be served with wholemeal bread either on its own or in the form of croutons.

Processes & Recipes — Starting Courses

Purée Soups — Vegetable

Yield — 5 portions

Process
1. Wash and, if necessary, peel the vegetables.
2. Cut vegetables into a small dice or slice.
3. Sweat vegetables in butter or oil.
4. Add liquid and seasoning.
5. Bring to the boil and skim as necessary.
6. Add thickening vegetable if required.
7. Simmer until tender.
8. Remove whole herbs.
9. Liquidise.
10. Serve with croutons (see basic preparations).

Vegetable Soup

500g	Vegetables, onion or carrot or fennel or leek or celery or mixed.
1.5l	White vegetable stock.
25g	Butter or 15ml olive oil.
	Sea salt and freshly ground pepper.
	Sprig of thyme and parsley.
½	Bay leaf.

Fresh Tomato Soup

400g	Ripe tomatoes.
1	Clove garlic.
5ml	Dry basil or sprig of fresh basil.
25g	Finely chopped onion.
1l	White vegetable stock.
25g	Chopped white of leek.
25g	Chopped celery.
	Sprig of thyme.
	Sea salt and freshly ground black pepper.

Suggested Complement
Serve on menus that contain pulses and cereals or dairy produce.

Processes & Recipes — Starting Courses

Whole Vegetable and Pulse Soups

Yield — 5 portions

Process
1. Wash and, if necessary, peel the vegetables.
2. (a) Cut vegetables into a small regular dice or slice, no bigger than 1cm square or cube.
   (b) For pulse soup, or if pulses are used, drain from cooking liquid.
3. Sweat vegetables in oil or butter until a small amount of juice is produced.
4. Add the three quarters cooked pulses and seasoning.
5. Cover with liquid, boil, skim and simmer for 20 mins.
6. Add pasta or potato, if used and continue cooking until tender.
7. Season and correct consistency.
8. Remove herbs, reboil, add pesto if used.
9. Serve. The soup may be garnished with grated cheese, chopped parsley or toasted cheese flutes.

Bean Soup
- 400g   Mixed or single variety of beans three-quarters cooked in unsalted water.
- 100g   Finely diced onion.
- 100g   Finely diced carrot.
- 50g   Finely diced celery.
- 15g   Chopped parsley.
         Sprig of thyme.
- ½   Bay leaf.
- 1l   White vegetable stock.
- 0.75l White bean cooking liquid.
- 2   Cloves crushed garlic.
- 15ml   Olive oil.
         Sea salt and freshly ground pepper to taste.

Processes & Recipes — Starting Courses

Vegetable Soup
- 500g Mixed vegetables — onion, swede, carrot, fennel, celery.
- 15g Chopped parsley.
-   Sprig thyme.
- ½ Bay leaf.
- 1.5l White vegetable stock.
- 15ml / 15g or Olive oil or butter.
-   Sea salt or freshly ground black pepper to taste.

Vegetable Soup with Pesto
- 400g Mixed vegetables — onion, leek, carrot, fennel, cabbage, celery, swede.
- 50g Wholewheat spaghetti, broken into 3cm lengths.
- 1.5l White vegetable stock.
- 30ml Pesto.
- 100g Diced ripe tomatoes.
- 30g Grated cheese.
- 15ml Olive oil.
-   Sea salt and freshly ground black pepper to taste.

Suggested Complement
Serve bean soups with wholemeal bread and cheese and vegetable soups with cheese.

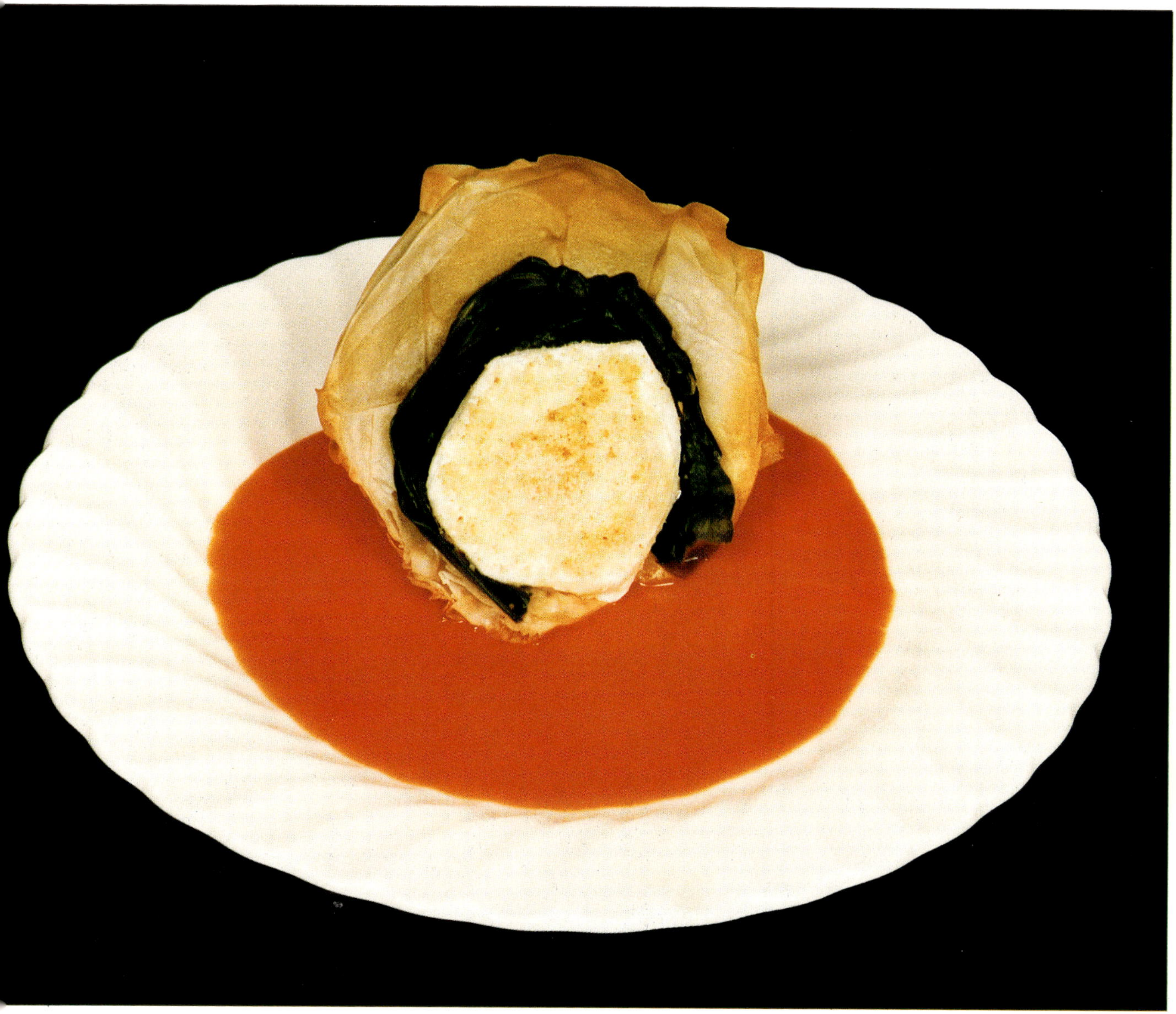

Processes & Recipes — Starting Courses

Egg & Souffle Dishes

Roulade

Yield — 5 portions

Process
1. Line a swiss roll tin with buttered paper.
2. Cook the main vegetable, refresh and squeeze dry.
3. Chop the dry vegetable in a food processor or liquidiser.
4. Mix the egg yolk, butter, liquidised vegetable and seasoning.
5. Whip the egg whites until stiff.
6. Fold in one-third of the egg white until smooth.
7. Fold in two-thirds of the egg white until smooth, without over beating.
8. Pour into the prepared swiss roll tray and spread to a thickness of 1cm.
9. Bake in a pre-heated oven at gas 5 (190°C) until the mixture is just brown, this should take 15-17 minutes.
10. Prepare the filling by mixing all ingredients together.
11. Turn out the mixture on to a tea towel covered with a sheet of greaseproof paper, cool.
12. Peel off the greaseproof paper (if it sticks cover with a damp tea towel).
13. Spread with filling and roll-up using the tea towel underneath.
14. Serve sliced with a sauce.

Spinach Roulade

    500g   Spinach.
    5   Egg yolks.
    15g   Soft butter.
    5   Egg whites.
            Sea salt and freshly ground black pepper.
            Filling
    30ml   Double cream.
    75ml   Basic white sauce.
    200g   Sliced and sweated mushrooms.
            Sea salt and freshly ground white pepper.
            Freshly ground nutmeg.

Suggested Complement
Serve with potato or whole grain rice.

Souffle

Yield — 5 portions

Process
1. Prepare the moulds by buttering the sides only.
2. Melt the butter in a thick bottom saucepan.
3. Add the flour and cook without colour.
4. Boil the milk with the salt.
5. Off the heat add the milk to the flour and butter and reboil.
6. Cool slightly.
7. Add egg yolks, main flavour ingredient and seasoning.
8. Stiffly whisk whites.
9. Add one-third of the whites to the cheese mixture and work to remove lumps.
10. Add one-third more of the whites and mix.
11. Add the remaining one-third of the whites and mix and pour into a prepared mould.
12. Cook at gas 6, 210°C for 10-15 minutes.
13. Serve immediately.

Cheese Souffle

7g	Butter for greasing moulds.
25g	Butter.
25g	Wholemeal Flour.
3	Yolks of egg.
4	Whites of egg.
50g	Grated vegetarian cheese.
300ml	Milk.

Sea salt, cayenne pepper and made English mustard.

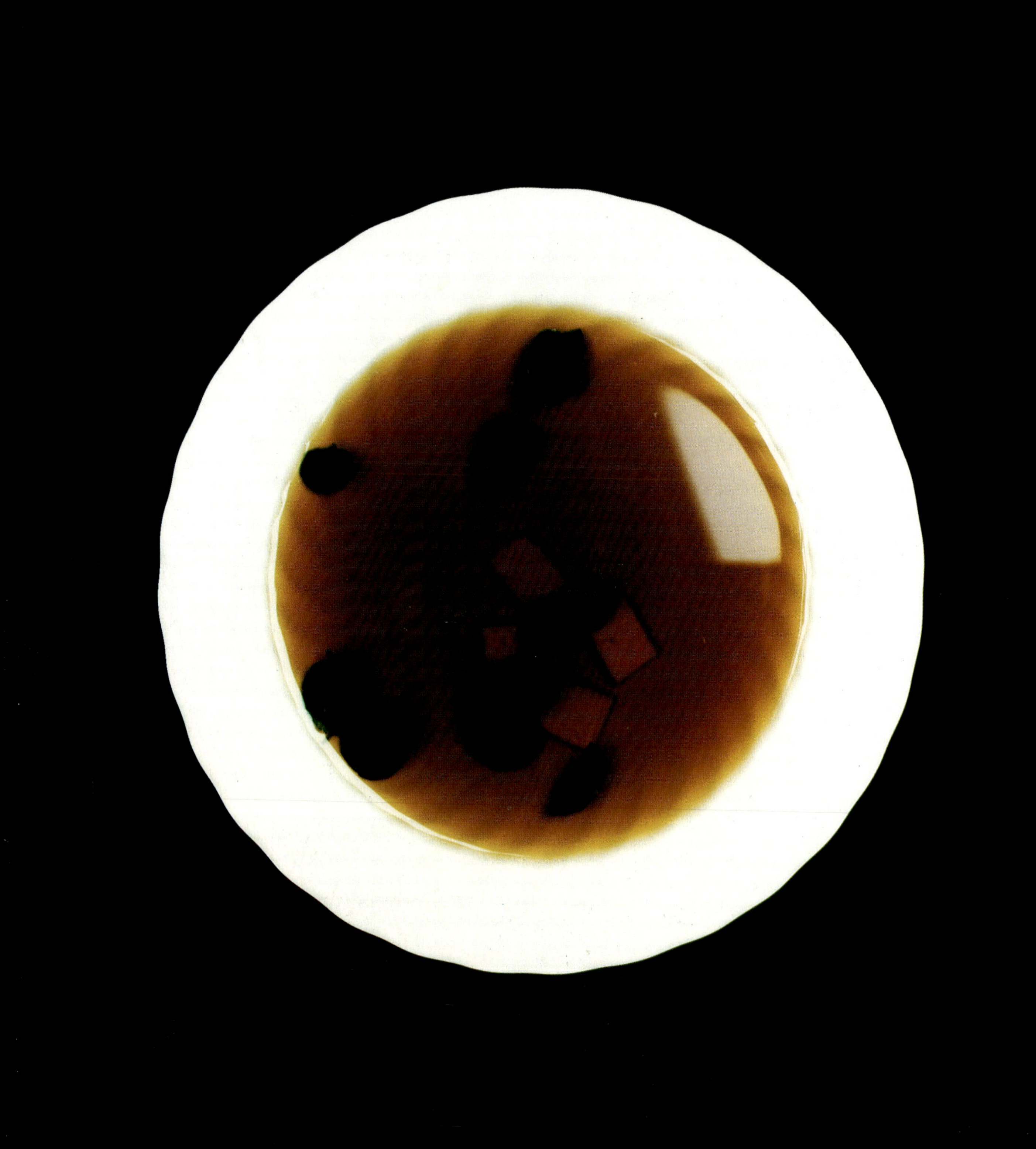

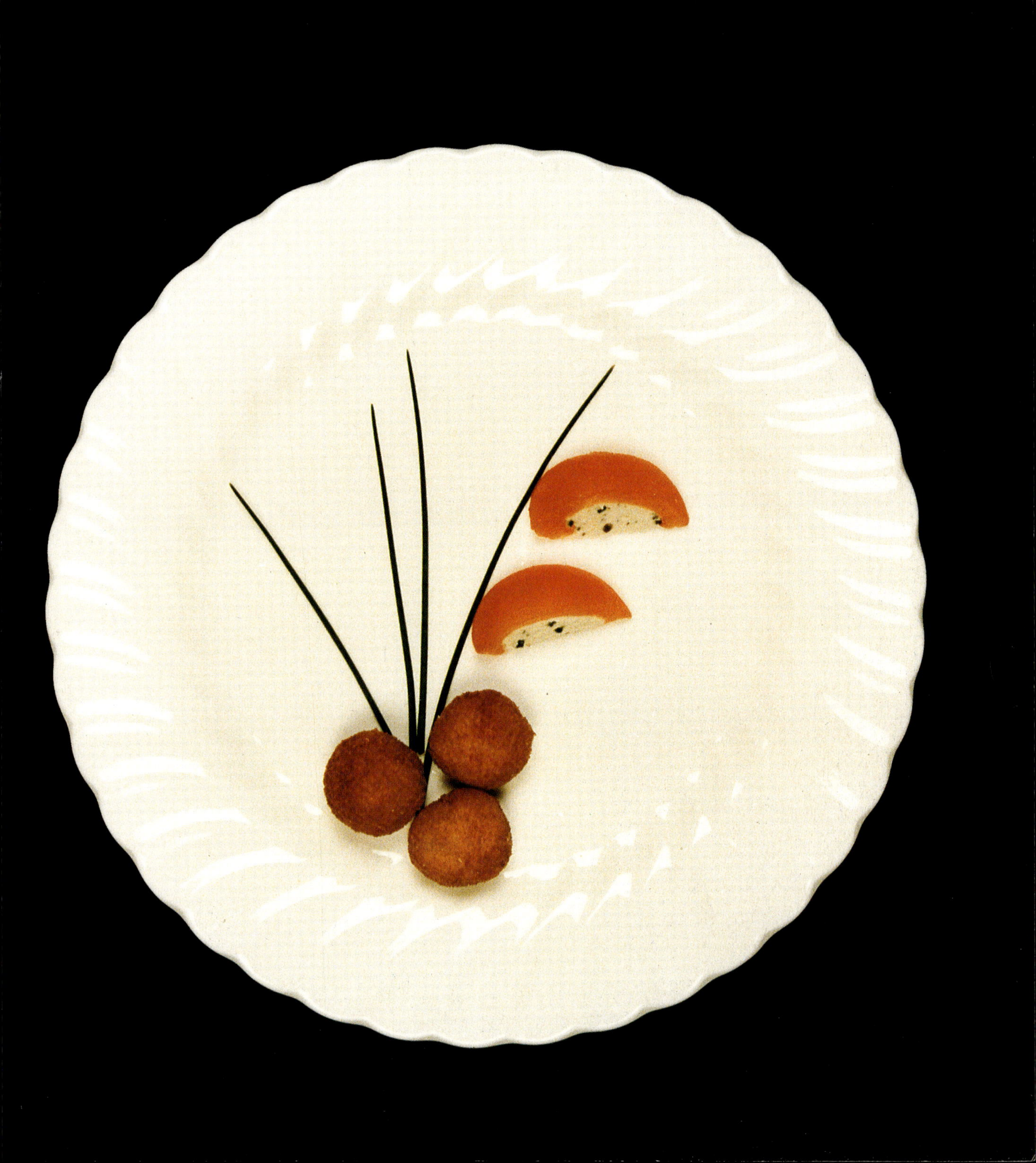

Processes & Recipes — Starting Courses

Spinach Souffle
- 7g   Butter for greasing moulds.
- 25g   Butter.
- 25g   Wholemeal flour.
- 3   Yolks of egg.
- 4   Whites of egg.
- 75g   Spinach Puree.
- 300ml Milk.
- Sea salt and nutmeg.

Leek or Broccoli Souffle
Replace spinach with Broccoli or leek puree.

Suggested Complement
Souffles are high in protein and will balance out most vegetable meals.

Scrambled Egg

Yield — 5 portions

Process
1. Beat the eggs in a mixing bowl.
2. Whisk until thoroughly mixed, and season then whisk again.
3. Heat a thick bottomed pan, add butter and melt.
4. Pour in the egg mix.
5. Add any cooked garnish.
6. Stir with a wooden spoon, scraping the setting egg from the sides and bottom of the pan.
7. When the mix is thick and creamy, cream may be added to hold the mix.
8. Serve immediately.

Scrambled Egg with Mushroom
- 10   Free range eggs.
- 20mls Double cream (optional).
- Sea salt and freshly ground pepper.
- 50g   Quartered button mushrooms (cooked).

Scrambled Egg with Courgettes and Olives

10	Free range eggs.
	Sea salt and freshly ground pepper.
1	Blanched de-seeded & diced tomato.
1	Small Courgette, diced and sautéd in butter.
3	Black olives stoned and cut in half.

Suggested Complement
Serve with or follow a simple salad.

Eggs in Cocotte

Yield — 5 portions

Process
1. Grease the cocottes with butter and season.
2. Add the cooked garnish to the cocotte.
3. Add the egg and season.
4. Poach in a bain-marie or water bath until the mixture is firm and the yolk cooked but soft.

Eggs in Cocotte with Tomato

5	Fresh free range eggs.
	Sea salt and freshly ground pepper.
25g	Butter.
50g	Diced, de-seeded tomato sauted in butter.

Eggs in Cocotte with Ratatouille

5	Fresh free range eggs.
	Sea salt and freshly ground pepper.
25g	Butter.
50g	Diced, cooked ratatouille (see stewed vegetables).

Suggested Complement
Serve with wholemeal bread and follow with a salad.

Processes & Recipes — Starting Courses

Poached Eggs

Yield — 5 portions

Process
1. Use a pan with approximately 10cm sides.
2. Three-quarters fill with water and add the vinegar.
3. Bring to the boil.
4. Break the egg into the hottest part of the liquid ie. where it is moving the most.
5. Baste the egg with a metal spoon in order to shape the white around the yolk as it was in the shell.
6. Remove after 3 minutes.
7. Drain on kitchen paper.
8. Serve coated with sauce on toast, bread or cooked vegetables.
9. Alternatively serve in a pre-cooked fillo pastry case (see photograph).

Poached Eggs with Cheese and Spinach
- 5 Fresh free range eggs.
- 100ml Basic white sauce (see basic preparation).
- 50g Grated vegetarian cheddar cheese.
- 200g Cooked dry spinach.
- Sea salt and freshly ground pepper.
- 15ml Vinegar.

Photograph on Page 129

Poached Eggs with Mushrooms and Sweetcorn
- 5 Fresh free range eggs.
- 100ml Basic white sauce (see basic preparation).
- 50g Sliced cooked mushrooms.
- 25g Cooked sweetcorn nibs.
- Sea salt and freshly ground pepper.
- 15ml Vinegar.

Suggested Complement
Follow with green salad and baked potato.

Processes & Recipes — Starting Courses

Stuffed Hard Boiled Eggs

Yield — 5 portions

Process
1. Using a small knife or special egg pricker put a small hole in the blunt end of the eggs (the hole helps prevent the shell from cracking).
2. Lower the eggs into fast boiling water.
3. Boil for 10 minutes.
4. Refresh under running cold water until completely cold.
5. Peel the eggs and cut lengthwise using a stainless steel knife (carbon steel knives will make the egg go black).
6. Remove the yolk and pass through a fine sieve.
7. Mix sieved egg with other filling and season.
8. Fill the egg with the mixture, shaping it to form a complete egg, half white, half filling.
9. Coat with sauce, if used, and reheat in the oven.

Eggs Chimay
- 5   Free range eggs.
- 300ml   Cheese sauce.

   Filling
- 25g   Finely chopped shallot.
- 125g   Finely chopped mushrooms sweated off.
- 5g   Butter.
- 5ml   Chopped Parsley.
           Sea salt and freshly ground black pepper.

Processes & Recipes — Starting Courses

Cottage Cheese and Red Pepper
    5   Free range eggs.

            Filling
    1   Small red pepper, finely chopped.
    100g   Drained cottage cheese.
    25g   Walnuts.
    5mls   Chopped chives.
            Sea salt and freshly ground black pepper.

Suggested Complement
Serve with or follow with salad and bread or baked potato.

Omelets

Yield — 5 portions

Process
1. Break the eggs into a basin.
2. Mix with a fork until thoroughly mixed, season and remix.
3. For flat omelets, add the garnish.
4. Prove an omelet pan, covering the base of the pan with salt and heating until the salt starts to go brown. Remove the salt and add *off heat* some cooking oil. Remove the oil.
5. Reheat the omelet pan and add the butter.
6. Pour in the egg mix.
7. Leave to set on the bottom for thirty seconds.
8. Shake the pan with the left hand and stir with the fork in the right hand.
9. When the eggs are set on the bottom but soft on top add the garnish.
10. For flat omelets put the pan under the grill to puff the egg and serve.
11. Tilt the pan and roll the omelet with the fork to form cigar shape.
12. Tip out onto a plate.
13. Garnish with some of the filling.

Processes & Recipes — Starting Courses

Vegetable Omelet
- 15   Fresh free range eggs.
-       Sea salt and freshly ground black pepper.
- 400g Cooked peas, sweetcorn, cooked potato diced, courgettes cooked and diced.

Suggested Complement
Serve with baked potato and salad or wholemeal pitta bread.

Savoury Flans

Yield — 4 portions

Process
1. Using savoury wholemeal pastry, line a 20cm flan ring (see flans — sweet section).
2. Beat eggs with seasoning.
3. Cover the bottom of the flan case with filling.
4. Add milk to beaten eggs and pour into flan case.
5. Bake at gas 4 180°C for 30 minutes or until egg mixture rises and pastry is golden brown.
6. Remove the flan ring and allow to cool.

Ingredients
- 150g Savoury wholemeal pastry.
- 1   Egg.
- 30g   Grated vegetarian cheddar cheese.
- 25g   Sliced and sweated mushrooms.
- 150ml Milk.
-       Sea salt and freshly ground black pepper.

CHAPTER 6
Processes & Recipes
Main Courses

The main course processes shown in this chapter are broken down into the following groups; Vegetables & Potatoes, Grains (ie Pasta, Rice & Breads), Pulses, Nuts & Seeds & Salads. Recipes are in most cases given for a yield of 5 covers giving an adequate portion size when the dish is used as a composite part of a 3 course meal. Caterers must consider this and where necessary adjust the recipe should the dish be used as a starter or a meal on its own. The applications shown for each process are not finite. Providing the basic process is used, caterers can vary the applications by using their imagination to suit their particular market preferences and the availability of commodities.

Vegetables & Potatoes

Stewed Vegetables, Vegetable Stroganoff, Stuffed Peppers, Vegetables with Cheese Sauce, Stir Fried Vegetables, Pot Roast Vegetables, Baked Sliced Potatoes, Baked Potatoes, Anna Style Potatoes, Purée Potatoes, Gaufrette

Stewed Vegetables

Yield — 5 covers

Process
1. Use a thick bottomed oven proof pan.
2. Heat the pan with oil and sweat the onions, garlic, and tough vegetables eg peppers.
3. Add the soft vegetables and other ingredients.
4. Cover with a tight fitting lid.
5. Place in the oven on 160°C, Gas 5, for 30 mins or until vegetables are soft.

Ratatouille
1	Large aubergine, sliced.
2	Large courgettes, sliced.
1	Green pepper, de-seeded and sliced.
1	Red pepper, de-seeded and sliced.
3	Cloves garlic, chopped.
4	Large tomatoes or 1 A2½ tin.
25ml	Cold pressed olive oil.
1	Med onion, peeled and sliced.
	Sea salt and freshly ground black pepper.

Okra with Tomatoes
500g	Okra, washed, topped and tailed and cut into 1cm lengths.
5	Tomatoes or 1 A2½ tin.
2	Cloves garlic, chopped.
20ml	Cold pressed olive oil.
1	Med onion, peeled and sliced.

Stewed Peas
500g	Frozen and fresh peas.
1	Lettuce, washed and shredded.
10	Button onions, peeled.
25g	Butter or 15ml olive oil.
10ml	Honey.

Suggested Complement
Serve with a nut roast or pasta dish.

Processes & Recipes — Main Courses

Vegetable Stroganoff

Yield — 5 portions

Process
1. Sweat onions in oil and add paprika.
2. Add prepared vegetables and cook until soft.
3. Add liquidised tofu and yoghurt.
4. Add mango chutney.
5. Bring just to the boil.
6. Season with cayenne pepper, sea salt and black pepper.
7. Serve with braised rice or pasta.

Mushroom Stroganoff
- 15ml Oil.
- 75g   Finely chopped onion.
- 500g Quartered mushrooms.
- 70ml Thick yoghurt.
- 80ml Silken tofu.
- 2g   Paprika.
- Pinch Cayenne pepper.
- 15ml Chopped mango chutney.

Courgette Stroganoff
As for mushroom stroganoff replacing mushrooms for washed and sliced courgettes.

Suggested Complement
Serve with whole wheat pasta or brown rice.

Processes & Recipes — Main Courses

Stuffed Peppers

Yield — 5 portions

Process
1. Wash the pepper.
2. Remove the stalk with a small knife by cutting the flesh around the base of the stalk.
3. Wash under fast running water to remove the seeds that remain.
4. Take a thin slice off the other end to enable the pepper to be stood up.
5. Prepare the filling.
6. Stuff the peppers with the filling.
7. Replace the stalk over the filling.
8. Place the peppers on a bed of sliced carrots, onions and celery in an oven proof pan.
9. Cover with tin foil.
10. Bake in an oven at gas 6, 200°C, for 45 mins.
11. Serve garnished with parsley.

Stuffed Peppers with Mushrooms & Almonds

5	Peppers.		
50g	Sliced sweated mushrooms	(	
5	Green or red peppers.	(	
25g	Finely chopped sweated onion.	(	
200g	Braised long grain Italian brown rice.	(	Filling.
50g	Blanched and roasted almonds.	(	
50g	Carrots	(	
50g	Onions	(Bed of sliced vegetables.	
2	Celery sticks	(	

Suggested Complement
Serve on a menu with a pulse or bean dish.

Processes & Recipes — Main Courses

Vegetables with a Cheese Sauce

Yield — 5 portions

Process
1. Boil or steam the vegetable until it is three quarters cooked.
2. Drain the vegetable.
3. Arrange the vegetable, either whole or portioned, in an oven proof dish.
4. Coat with sauce.
5. Sprinkle with grated cheese.
6. Place under a grill or into a hot oven to re-heat and brown.

Cauliflower Cheese
- 1 Large cauliflower.
- 500ml Basic white sauce with the addition of:
- 30ml Double cream or yoghurt
- 5ml Made English mustard
- Pinch Cayenne pepper.
- 100g Grated vegetarian cheese.

Broccoli Cheese
- 750g Fresh broccoli.
- 500ml Sauce as for cauliflower cheese.

Leeks in Cheese Sauce
- 750g Leeks.
- 500ml Sauce as for cauliflower cheese.

Suggested Complement
Serve with baked potatoes in their jackets.

Stir Fried Vegetables

Yield — 5 portions

Process
1. Heat a wok (see Methods of Cookery).
2. Add the hard or tough vegetables to the hot wok.
3. Add other ingredients and stir over a fierce heat for 1-2 minutes.
4. Serve immediately.

Stir Fried Vegetables in a Basket
- 500g Large potatoes, peeled and cut for gaufrettes, overlapped into a wire basket and deep fried until crisp at a temperature of 150°C to produce a basket approximately 10-15cm across.

Photograph on Page 153

Vegetables
- 500g Mixed prepared vegetables eg: mange-tout, french beans, baby sweetcorn, baby carrots, chanterelle, tomato (blanched and quartered and de-seeded), courgettes, okra, aubergine.

Pot Roast Vegetables

Yield — 5 portions

Process
1. Wash and, if necessary, peel vegetables.
2. Cut vegetables into fine strips approximately 3mm square by 7cm long.
3. Season and sweat vegetables in olive oil for 2-3 minutes.
4. Cover with a tight fitting lid.
5. Cook in an oven gas 4, 180°C, for 30-45 minutes.
6. Serve, garnished with chopped parsley if used.

Processes & Recipes — Main Courses

Pot Roast Red Pepper & Parsnips
- 450g   Parsnips.
- 2   Med. red peppers.
- 10ml   Olive oil.
- 15ml   Chopped parsley.
            Sea salt and freshly ground black pepper.

Pot Roast Green Pepper & Carrot
- 450g   Carrots.
- 2   Med. green peppers.
- 10ml   Olive oil.
- 15ml   Chopped parsley.
            Sea salt and freshly ground black pepper.

Pot Roast Courgettes
- 250g   Yellow courgettes.
- 250g   Green courgettes.
- 10ml   Olive oil.
            Sea salt and freshly ground white pepper.

Baked Sliced Potatoes

Yield — 5 portions

Process
1. Slice peeled raw potatoes by hand or using a mandolin.
2. Arrange slices in an ovenproof dish, alternating with other vegetables.
3. Add liquid to just below the top layer of potato and sprinkle with cheese if used.
4. Bake in a hot oven, gas 7, 220°C, for 20 minutes. Reduce heat to gas 3, 170°C, for a further hour until potatoes are cooked.
5. Serve in the dish sprinkled with chopped parsley.

Processes & Recipes — Main Courses

Baker's Style Potatoes
- 500g Sliced potatoes (King Edwards).
- 300ml Basic brown stock.
- 225g Sliced sweated onions or blanched leeks.
- 25g   Chopped parsley.
- Sea salt and freshly ground black pepper.

Swiss Style Potatoes
- 500g Sliced potatoes (King Edwards).
- 300ml Milk.
- 125g Grated vegetarian cheddar cheese.
- Sea salt and freshly ground white pepper.
- 25g   Chopped parsley.

Baked Potatoes

Yield — 5 portions

Process
1. Use medium sized potatoes, approximately 150g in weight.
2. Scrub to remove all dirt.
3. Using a small knife, remove any eye's or blemishes.
4. For a soft skin rub the potato with sunflower oil.
5. Cut the potato along the top to form a cross.
6. Place on a bakingsheet covered in salt for a crisp potato. Do not use salt if the potato has been oiled.
7. Bake in an oven at 200°C, gas 6, for 45-60 minutes until the potatoes are soft to the 'pinch'.
8. Using the thumb and first finger of each hand pinch-up the cut to produce a pocket for the filling.

Fillings
Cottage cheese and chives, grated vegetarian cheddar cheese, sour cream, finely diced stir fried vegetables.

Processes & Recipes — Main Courses

Anna Style Potatoes

Yield — 5 portions

Process
1. Take even sized potatoes (King Edwards).
2. Wash and peel.
3. Slice very finely, using a mandolin.
4. Heat an Anna mould or heavy omelet pan with a small amount of oil or oil and butter.
5. Dry the sliced potato and season with salt, pepper and nutmeg.
6. Neatly arrange the potato slices in the hot pan.
7. Alternate the potatoes with other vegetables in the centre if used.
8. Finish with potato slices and press down with the back of a metal spoon and top with butter.
9. Bake in the oven at gas 6, 200°C, for 30-40 minutes, pressing the potatoes down regularly.
10. Turn out and drain off surplus oil or butter.
11. Garnish with chopped parsley.

Anna Potatoes

  500g Sliced dry potatoes.
  50g Butter or oil.
  25g Chopped Parsley.

Additional Ingredients
  50g Grated vegetarian cheese, sliced cooked mushrooms, sliced red pepper, cooked dry spinach.

Potatoes Gaufrettes

Yield — 5 portions

Wash, peel and re-wash the medium sized potatoes.
 Cut on the serrated blade of a mandolin or hand-vegetable slicer. Rotate the potato through 90°C and repeat to produce thin potato slices with lattice holes.

Processes & Recipes — Main Courses

Purée Potatoes

Yield — 5 portions

Process
1. Wash and peel the potatoes.
2. Cook in salted water until soft.
3. Drain off the water and heat the potatoes to remove any surplus moisture.
4. Using a coarse sieve or potato ricer, mash the potato.
5. Add other ingredients.
6. Pipe or mould as necessary.

Duchess Potato
- 500g Potatoes.
- 1 Yolk of egg.
- Freshly ground nutmeg, sea salt and white pepper.

Pipe into domes, 3cm wide by 5cm high, brush with egg wash and bake until golden brown.

Marquise Potatoes
- 600g Duchess mix.

Pipe into nests 5cm round, brush with egg wash and bake until golden brown.
Fill with diced cooked tomato or other stir-fried vegetables.

Dauphine Potatoes
- 500g Duchess Mixture.
- 150ml Choux Paste Mixture.

Combine both mixtures and spoon mould (see spoon moulding) into egg shapes. Deep fry 250°C until golden brown.

Other vegetables may be added to the Dauphine mixture at the rate of 50g per 500g mix. Example of vegetables: cooked spinach, cooked red pepper.

Processes & Recipes — Main Courses

Grains

Vegetarian Suet Pudding, Raised Pie — Nut and Vegetable Filling, Chick-pea and Pepper Couscous, Savoury Fillo Cake, Quick Bread, Pizza, Pitta Bread, Naan Bread, Pasta Dumplings, Spaghetti with Sauces, Noodles with Sauces, Blini with Leeks and Mushrooms, Cottage Cheese Lasagna, Rice Cakes, Braised Millet, Braised Brown Rice

Vegetarian Suet Pudding

Yield — 5 portions

Process
1. Prepare and three quarters cook the filling by sweating in a large saucepan.
2. Use a 200g flour mix of vegetarian suet pastry.
3. Line a 1 litre (2 pt) pudding basin or five individual pudding moulds with two-thirds of the pastry and brush the edge with water.
4. Fill with prepared filling.
5. Roll out the remaining one third pastry for the lid.
6. Cover filling, crimp edges and protect with tin-foil.
7. Steam for 1½ hours at low pressure or 1 hour at high pressure.

Photograph on Page 157

Aduki Bean and Mushroom Pudding

200g	Flour mix of vegetarian suet pastry.
100g	Cooked aduki beans.
100g	Cooked mushrooms.
100g	Diced tomato.
100g	Diced courgette.
50g	Diced potato.
50g	Finely chopped and sweated onion.
30ml	Shoyu.
20ml	Chopped parsley,
	sprig Chopped sage.
15ml	Red wine.
	Sea salt and freshly ground black pepper.

Suggested Complement
Serve with baked potatoes and fresh salad.

Nut and Vegetable Pie Filling

Use a 450g flour mixture of hot water pastry.

1	Large green pepper de-seeded, diced and sweated with onion.
100g	Finely chopped onion, sweated.
25g	Butter.
225g	Hazelnuts or cooked chestnuts.
100g	Cooked continental lentils.
5ml	Mixed herbs.
5ml	Shoyu.
2	Beaten eggs (optional).
100g	Cooked, quartered mushrooms sweated with onion.
225g	Blanched brussel sprouts.
50g	Leek chopped and sweated with onion.
	Sea salt and freshly ground black pepper.

This recipe may be changed by replacing the continental lentils with cooked beans and the Brussel Sprouts with another vegetable.

Suggested Complement
The combination of wheat pastry and pulse make the pie reasonably well balanced.

Raised Pies

Yield — 8 portions

Process
1. Prepare the filling by combining all the ingredients.
2. Prepare the mould by greasing with vegetable fat or butter.
3. Make Hot Water Pastry (see Basic Preparations).
4. Line the mould while the pastry is hot, leaving one third of the pastry for the lid.
5. Fill the lined mould with prepared filling.
6. Brush the edge of the pastry with beaten egg or water.
7. Attach lid and decorate.
8. Brush with egg wash.
9. Bake in an oven at gas 5, 190°C, for 40-60 minutes depending on the filling.
10. Remove from the oven and allow to cool for 15 minutes.
11. Remove from the mould and serve hot or cold.

Processes & Recipes — Main Courses

Chick-pea and Pepper Couscous

Yield — 5 portions

Process
1. Soak the chick-peas overnight.
2. Prepare and cut the vegetables into a large dice but leave the potatoes whole.
3. Fry the peppers, onions, aubergine, courgette, turnip and carrot in the olive oil, using the bottom of a double boiler.
4. Add the chilli, paprika and seasoning and fry for 2-3 minutes.
5. Add the potatoes and chick-peas.
6. Add the tomatoes and water and bring to the boil.
7. Wet the couscous with a little cold water and place in the top of a double boiler. *Do not pack.*
8. Cook the couscous for 35-40 minutes from the time steam starts to rise through the grain.
9. Remove the top of the double boiler and empty the couscous into a bowl and sprinkle generously with water to break up the lumps; keep warm.
10. Finish cooking the vegetables.
11. Serve the couscous mixed with cinnamon and arrange to form a bed, with the vegetables on top.

Ingredients

400g	Couscous.	30g	Turnip.
2	Med. red peppers.	250g	Tomatoes.
2	Med. green peppers.	30g	Carrot.
1	Large aubergine.	10g	Paprika.
1	Med. courgette.	3g	Powdered cinnamon.
1	Chilli pepper.	50ml	Olive oil.
250g	Finely chopped onion.	1l	Water.
100g	Chick-peas.		
100g	New potatoes with their skins on.		

Sea salt and freshly ground black pepper and nutmeg.

Suggested Complement
Serve with salad and pitta bread.

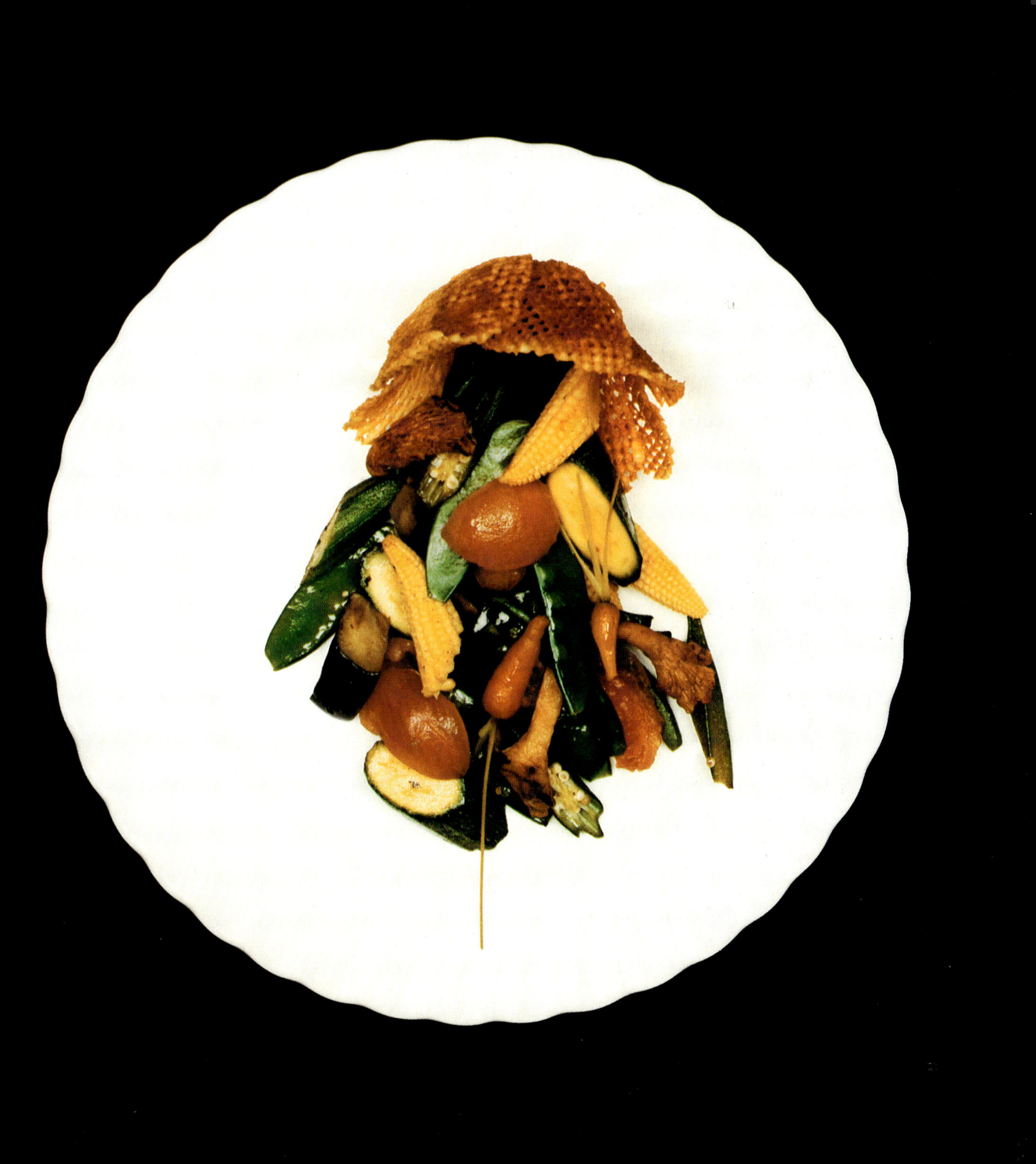

Processes & Recipes — Main Courses

Savoury Fillo Cake

Yield — 5 portions

Process
1. Prepare and cook the vegetable filling; if a leaf vegetable like spinach is used, squeeze to remove all moisture.
2. Mix eggs and seasoning.
3. Combine egg mixture with cooked vegetables and, if used, cheese.
4. Grease with butter or oil a spring loaded 23cm sponge tin or Anna mould.
5. Line with fillo pastry, leaving 5cm overlapping the edge.
6. Cover the bottom with vegetable and egg mixture.
7. Cover mixture with fillo pastry; continue alternating layers and sprinkling with green pepper corns.
8. Fold over the overlapping side leaves.
9. Brush with oil or melted butter.
10. Cook at gas 4, 180°C for 40-45 minutes.

Ingredients
- 200g Cooked vegetables; spinach or leeks or sweetcorn and red pepper or spinach and mushroom.
- 2 Beaten eggs.
- 100g Grated vegetarian Cheddar or Cottage Cheese.
- 100g Prepared Fillo pastry.
- 10g Green pepper corns.
- 25g Butter or 20ml sesame oil.
- Sea salt and freshly ground black pepper and nutmeg.

Suggested complement
Serve with salad and baked potatoes.

Photograph on Page 160

Pizza

Yield — 5 portions

Process
1. Dissolve the yeast in water and leave to froth.
2. Add salt, herbs and olive oil to the flour.
3. Add the yeast mixture to flour and knead to a smooth dough.
4. Grease a pizza tin.
5. Roll out the dough to fill the tin.
6. Prove to double size.
7. Prepare the filling by sweating onions, garlic and olive oil.
8. Add all the vegetables eg. mushrooms, courgettes, aubergines and sweat for 5 minutes.
9. Add tomatoes, herbs and tomato purée.
10. Reduce by a quarter and season with salt and pepper.
11. Bake the dough in a hot oven 225°C, gas 7 for 10 minutes
12. Remove the dough from the oven and coat with vegetable filling, olives and grated cheese.
13. Continue baking for 20 minutes.

Dough

300g	Wholemeal flour.
200ml	Warm water.
15g	Fresh yeast.
5ml	Olive oil.
2.5g	Sea salt.
5ml	Oregano.
5ml	Basil.

Processes & Recipes — Main Courses

Topping
- 1 × A 2½ Italian tomatoes *or* 500g ripe blanched tomatoes.
- 100g Finely chopped onion.
- 50mls Tomato purée.
- 5mls Oregano.
- 5mls Basil.
- 10 Stoned black olives.
- 250g Sliced mushrooms.
- 1 Courgette, sliced.
- 250g Grated vegetarian cheese.

Add other vegetables such as aubergines and blanched asparagus.

Suggested Complement
Serve with a fresh green salad.

Quick Bread

Yield — 2 loaves

Process
1. Add yeast to the flour and mix.
2. Add the other ingredients.
3. Knead to a smooth dough.
4. Divide into 2 loaves and place in greased tins.
5. Set to prove double size.
6. Bake in an oven at 225°C, gas 7, for 35 minutes.

Ingredients
- 1kg Whole meal flour.
- 2 Sachet quick blend yeast.
- 25g Butter.
- 600ml Warm water 45°C.
- 14g Sea salt, 2 tsp.

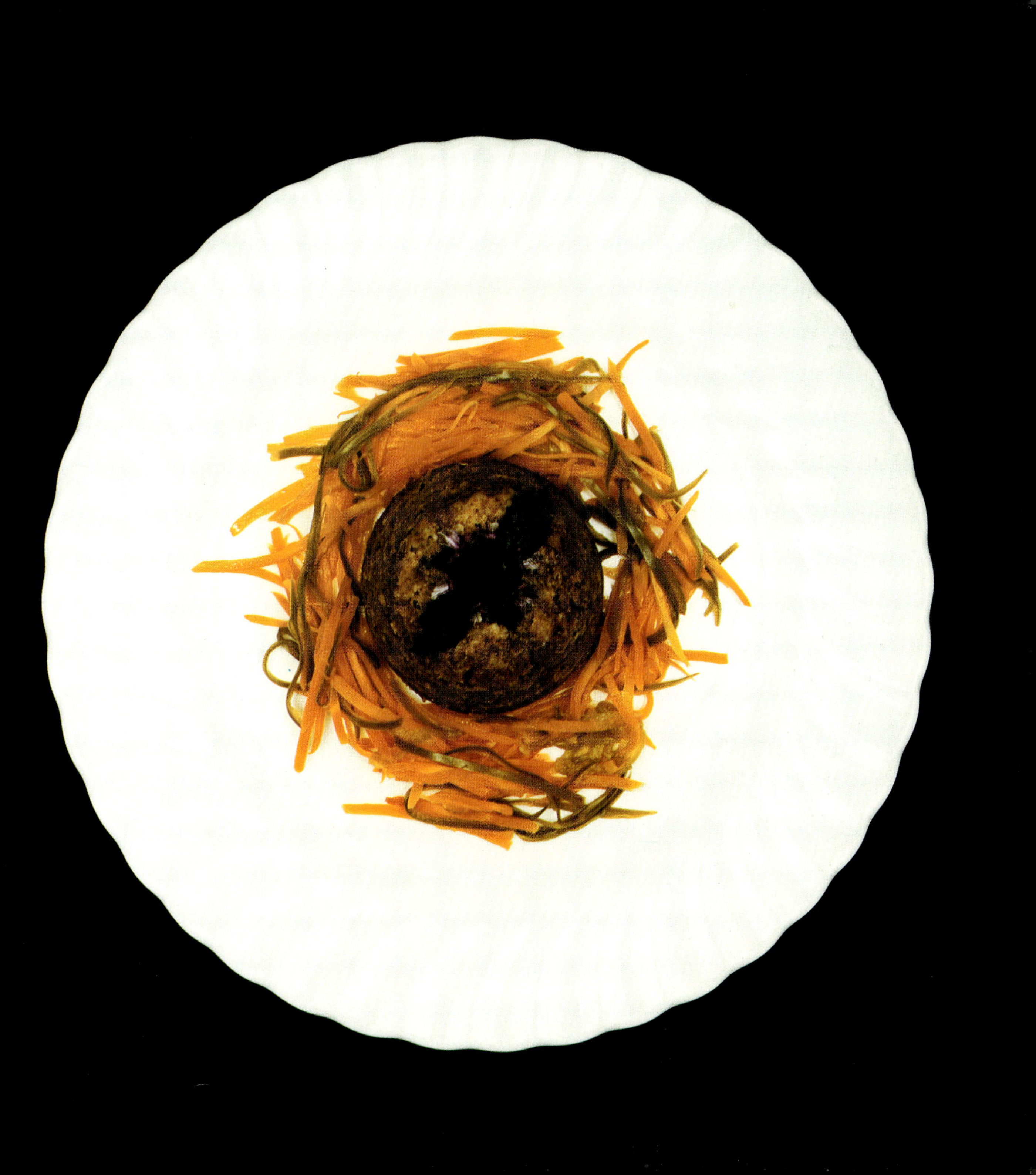

Processes & Recipes — Main Courses

Pitta Bread

Yield — 10 portions

Process
1. Dissolve yeast and sugar in water and leave until a froth forms.
2. Add salt to the flour.
3. Add liquid yeast mixture to the flour and knead to a smooth dough.
4. Cover with a damp cloth or place in a polythene bag, prove in a warm place to double size.
5. Divide the dough into 10 pieces.
6. Mould into balls and roll out into flat oval shapes.
7. Leave on a floured table to crust over and puff to double thickness.
8. Bake in an oven for 8-10 minutes at 225°C, gas 7.
9. Cover with a cloth to keep soft.

Ingredients
- 500g   Wholemeal flour.
- 15g   French yeast.
- 15g   Brown sugar.
- 15g   Salt.
- 350ml Warm water, 45°C.

Suggested Complement
Serve with dairy or bean based products.

Naan Bread

Yield — 10 portions

Process
1. Dissolve yeast and sugar in milk until a froth forms.
2. Add salt to the flour.
3. Add liquid yeast mixture, beaten egg and yoghurt to the flour and knead to a smooth slack dough.
4. Mould into a ball, rub with oil and leave to prove, double size.
5. Mould the mixture into 10 equal balls and roll out into oval shapes.
6. Heat the oven to 300°C, gas 10.
7. Heat a baking sheet in the oven.
8. Place naans on the hot sheet and bake in the oven until the dough puffs and turns golden brown.
9. Cover with a cloth to keep warm and soft.

Ingredients
- 200ml Blood heat milk or soya milk.
- 10g   Brown sugar.
- 25g   Fresh yeast.
- 500g   Strong flour
- 1   Beaten egg, substitute with soya milk for vegan diet.
- 5g   Salt.
- 150ml Plain yoghurt, substitute with silken tofu for vegan diet.
- 30ml   Sunflower oil.

Suggested Complement
Serve with a bean based curry.

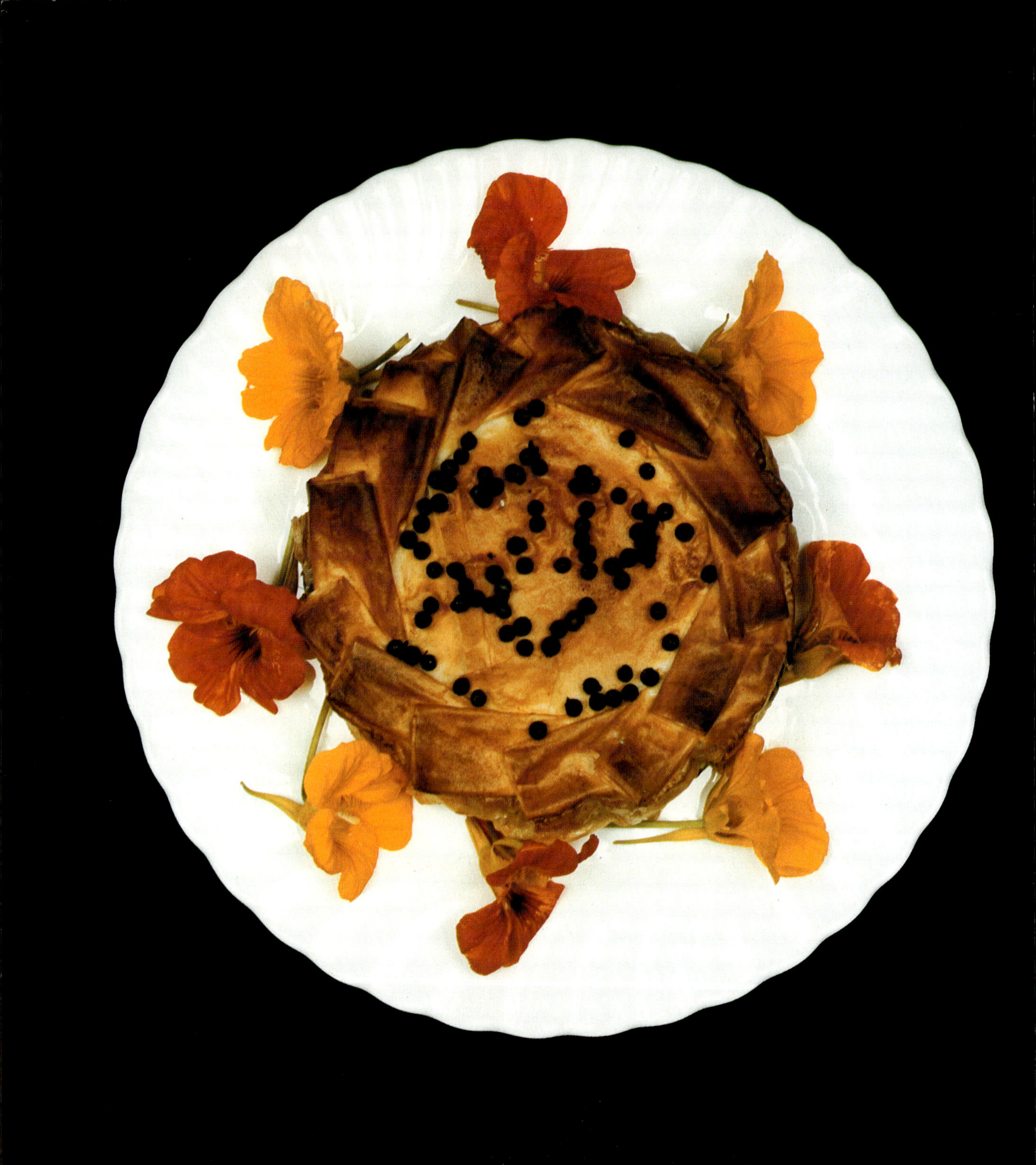

Processes & Recipes — Main Courses

Pasta Dumplings

Yield — 5 portions

Process
1. Roll out the noodle pastry into 12cm squares.
2. Brush with water or beaten egg.
3. Place the prepared filling in the centre.
4. Fold the pastry over the filling and seal to form an envelope.
5. Poach the dumpling in a shallow pan of simmering, salted water for 15-20 minutes.
6. Remove the dumplings with a perforated spoon and drain.
7. Place the cooked dumplings in a greased earthern-ware dish.
8. Coat with prepared sauce — Tomato — Pepper etc.
9. Sprinkle with a hard vegetarian cheese and brown in the oven.

Ingredients
50g	Grated vegetarian cheddar cheese.
2	Cloves of garlic crushed and puréed.
100g	Cooked purée of mushroom.
25g	Wholewheat breadcrumbs.
50g	Cooked leaf spinach.
100g	Flour mix of noodle dough.
	Sea salt, freshly ground nutmeg and black pepper.

Suggested Complement
Serve on a menu with beans or pulses and salad.

Processes & Recipes — Main Courses

Spaghetti with Sauce

Process
1. To cook wholemeal spaghetti it is advisable to use 2 litres of boiling salted water to 500g of spaghetti.
2. Add 30ml of oil to each 2 litres of water in order to prevent the spaghetti from sticking together.
3. Cook the spaghetti for 15-20 minutes on a fast boil.
4. The cooked spaghetti should still retain a bite.
5. Drain the spaghetti.
6. Heat some pesto (see Basic Preparations), butter or olive oil with sea salt, freshly ground black pepper and nutmeg in a large saucepan.
7. Add to cooked spaghetti to reheat and gain flavour.
8. Add one third of the sauce and mix with the spaghetti.
9. Serve in an entrée dish with the remaining sauce.

Suggested Sauces
Tomato sauce with a dice of tomato. Allow 300ml of sauce to 100g of raw spaghetti.

Suggested Complement
Serve on a menu with pulses or dairy products.

Noodles with Sauces

Yield — 5 portions

Process
1. Prepare the noodles by rolling the pastry (see Basic Preparation), thin enough to see your hand through.
2. Cut the pastry into a rough oblong.
3. Dust well with flour or semolina.
4. Fold into 4.
5. Using a large sharp knife cut across the end of the pastry to produce ribbons 5cm wide.
6. Keep the noodles one layer deep on a tray sprinkled with flour or semolina.
7. Cook in a saucepan containing 5 times the amount of water to pasta.
8. Bring the water to a rapid boil and add sea salt and oil (to prevent sticking).
9. Add noodles, stirring with a fork to prevent sticking.
10. Cook for 10 minutes, drain and combine with pesto and sauce.

Suggested Sauces
Tomato (see Basic Preparation).

Mushroom and Cheese
- 100g   Sliced sweated mushrooms simmered with:
- 200ml Double Cream
    Sea salt, freshly ground black pepper and nutmeg.

Suggested Complement
Serve on a menu with pulses or dairy produces.

Blini with Leeks and Mushrooms

Yield — 5 portions

Process
1. Make pancake batter.
2. Wash and finely shred the leeks.
3. Sweat the leeks in butter.
4. Add cream and seasoning and reduce to double thickness.
5. Turn 5 mushrooms and cook them in oil.
6. Finely chop red pepper.
7. Quarter the remaining mushrooms.
8. Sweat the mushrooms, onion and pepper.
9. Mould the leek mixture into egg shapes.
10. Fry the pancakes.
11. Split the pancakes and fill with pepper and mushroom mixture.
12. Dress on a plate with leek shapes and watercress.
13. Garnish each pancake with a turned mushroom.

Ingredients

75g	Buckwheat flour mix of Blini batter.
4	Leeks.
1	Med. red pepper.
40g	Finely chopped onion.
20mls	Double cream.
	Sea salt and freshly ground black pepper.
5g	Butter or oil.
	Watercress for garnish.

Suggested Complement
Serve with a bean based salad.

Cottage Cheese Lasagna

Yield — 5 portions

Process
1. Using at least 3 times the amount of boiling salted water to lasagne, cook the lasagne until it is just cooked and still retaining a bite.
2. In a large oven proof dish place one quarter of the spinach and cottage cheese.
3. Season and add lemon juice.
4. Cover with cooked lasagna, repeat the filling etc, then lasagna.
5. Finish with lasagna.
6. Cover the top with cream, chopped nuts and grated vegetarian cheese.
7. Bake in the oven at gas 6, 200°C, for 30-40 minutes.
8. Remove from the oven and allow to rest for 15 minutes before cutting.
9. Serve with tomato sauce.

Ingredients
- 200g Wholemeal lasagna.
- 200g Spinach.
- 500ml Tomato sauce (see Basic Preparation).
- 150g Cottage cheese.
- 150g Grated vegetarian cheddar cheese.
-        Sea salt and freshly ground black pepper and nutmeg.
- 50g   Chopped mixed nuts.
- 50ml Double cream.
- 15ml Lemon juice.

Suggested Complement
Serve with salad.

Processes & Recipes — Main Courses

Rice Cakes with Spinach & Sweetcorn

Yield — 5 portions

Process
1. Braise the rice (see Braised Rice).
2. Cook, drain and chop the spinach.
3. Blanch the frozen sweetcorn or drain the tinned sweetcorn.
4. Beat the eggs and grate the vegetarian cheese.
5. Mix all the ingredients together.
6. Place a 7cm metal pastry cutter in a frying pan — add oil and heat.
7. Drop a tablespoon of the mixture into the cutter and fry until golden brown on the side, remove the cutter and turn the cake over.
8. Repeat until all the mixture is used up.

Ingredients

200g	Cooked long grain rice.
100g	Cooked sweetcorn nibs.
100g	Cooked spinach.
50g	Grated vegetarian cheddar.
3	Eggs beaten.
	Sea salt and freshly ground black pepper and nutmeg.

Suggested Complement
Serve with a salad.

Braised Millet

Yield — 5 portions

Process
1. In the minimum amount of oil sauté the millet to bring out the flavour, or toast under the grill.
2. Add brown vegetable stock and bring to the boil, simmer covered with a lid for 15 minutes.
3. Adjust the seasoning and finish with tamari.

Ingredients
- 300g Millet.
- 1l   Brown vegetable stock (see Basic Preparations).
- 20ml Tamari.
-       Sea salt and freshly ground black pepper and nutmeg.
- 5ml   Powdered marjoram.

Braised Brown Rice

Yield — 5 portions

Process
1. Fry the onions until they are golden brown.
2. Add the rice and fry for 1 minute.
3. Season and add the liquid.
4. Cover with a lid, bring to the boil and cook in the oven for 40-50 minutes.

Ingredients
- 300g   Washed and picked over brown rice.
- 600ml Brown vegetable stock (see Basic Preparations).
- 50g   Finely chopped onion.
- 15ml   Olive oil.
-        Sea salt and freshly ground black pepper and nutmeg.
- 5ml   Powdered marjoram.
- 5ml   Shoyu.

Suggested Complement
Serve with a pulse or diary dish.

Processes & Recipes — Main Courses

Pulses

Savoury Crumble, Bean and Vegetable Pancakes, Bean Bags, Bean Stews — Goulash — Curry, Nut and Pulse Cakes

Savoury Crumble

Yield — 5 portions

Process
1. Prepare basic filling — bean curry, ratatouille etc.
2. Mix all crumble ingredients together.
3. Three quarters fill an oven-proof dish with filling.
4. Top with crumble mix.
5. Bake gas 6, 200°C, for 30 minutes.

Crumble Mixture
- 100g   Wholemeal flour.
- 10g   Millet flakes.
- 10g   Sesame seeds.
- 50g   Chopped nuts (almonds, brazils, hazel, walnuts).
- 50ml   Olive oil or sesame oil.
- 10g   Grated vegetarian cheese (optional).
-        Sea salt, freshly ground black pepper and nutmeg.

Suggested Complement
Serve with a potato and pulse salad.

Bean and Vegetable Pancakes

Yield — 5 portions

Process
1. Cook the bean filling.
2. Prepare and cook the pancakes.
3. Fill the pancakes with the bean mixture.
4. Fold the pancakes to make a money bag, 3 cornered fold or roll.
5. Coat the base of the oven proof dish with the sauce.
6. Place the filled pancakes on the sauce and reheat in a hot oven.

Bean Bags with Red Pepper Sauce
- 500ml   Red pepper sauce.
- 125g   Flour mix or pancakes.
- 250g   Cooked bean goulash.

Rolled Curried Pancakes
- 500ml   Curry Sauce.
- 125g   Flour mix of pancakes.
- 250g   Blackeye bean curry.

Bean Bags Using Fillo Pastry

Yield — 5 portions

Process
1. Cook the bean filling — Bean Goulash, Curry etc.
2. Place a double sheet of Fillo pastry 25cm square on the table.
3. Place a portion of the filling in the centre of the square.
4. Fold to form a money-bag shape.
5. Bake in a hot oven 200°C until the pastry turns golden brown.
6. Serve on a plate coated with a sauce eg. red pepper.
7. Garnish with water cress or parsley.

Photograph on Page 177

Suggested Complement
Serve with a grain dish and green salad.

Processes & Recipes — Main Courses

Bean Stews

Yield — 5 portions

Process
1. Soak the beans overnight and drain.
2. Cover the soaked beans with water or stock, bring to the boil and simmer until tender.
3. Heat oil in an oven proof pan big enough to contain all ingredients.
4. Fry onion until golden brown.
5. Add garlic (if used) and spices, very lightly fry.
6. Add other vegetables — mushroom, tomatoes, courgettes, okra, spinach.
7. Simmer for 5 minutes.
8. Season with salt and pepper and add yoghurt.
9. Add beans to fried mixture, simmer in the oven 25 minutes.
10. Serve with chopped parsley or coriander.

Bean Goulash

225g	Beans — blackeyed, haricot, kidney.
1l	Water or vegetable stock.
225g	Mushrooms washed and sliced.
30ml	Oil.
150g	Onion peeled and chopped.
2	Cloves garlic peeled and chopped.
400g	Tomatoes peeled and chopped.
5g	Sea salt.
2g	Freshly ground black pepper.
10g	Paprika.
15ml	Chopped parsley.

Bean Curry

225g	Beans — haricots, kidney, blackeyed.
1l	Vegetable stock or water.
100g	Mushrooms washed and quartered.
100g	Okra washed, topped and tailed or spinach, washed.
30ml	Oil.
3	Cloves garlic peeled and chopped.
150g	Onion peeled and chopped.
400g	Tomatoes peeled and chopped.
5g	Sea salt.
4g	Ground cumin.
2g	Ground coriander.
2g	Turmeric.
2cm	Stick cinnamon ground.
1 or 2	Green chillies finely chopped.
15ml	Chopped coriander.
5g	Peeled and shredded fresh ginger.
150g	Plain yoghurt.

Suggested Complement
Serve with wholegrain cereal or pasta.

Processes & Recipes — Main Courses

Nut & Pulse Cakes

Yield — 5 portions

Process
1. Cook the pulses and sweat the onions, garlic and green pepper.
2. Grind the nuts in a liquidiser.
3. Mix ground nuts and other ingredients to form a paste and mould into cakes 7cm in diameter and 1cm thick.
4. Coat in flour, beaten egg and breadcrumbs.
5. Shallow fry until golden brown on both sides.

Green Lentil & Mixed Nut Cake
- 100g Wholemeal flour.
- 150g Cooked pulses.
- 100g Mixed nuts.
- 15g Finely chopped green pepper.
- 1 Clove garlic, finely chopped.
- 15g Finely chopped onion.
-   Cayenne pepper, ground nutmeg and sea salt.
- 2 Eggs.
- 200g Wholemeal breadcrumbs.

Suggested Complement
Serve with pitta bread or wholemeal rolls or a rice dish.

Nuts and Seeds

Nut and Vegetable Strudel, Millet and Nut Croquettes, Nut Loaf — Walnut and Green Peppercorn

Nut & Vegetable Strudel

Yield — 5 portions

Process
1. Combine the three quartered, cooked vegetables with the chopped nuts and other ingredients.
2. Place a double layer of fillo pastry on a sheet of grease proof paper.
3. Brush with melted butter.
4. Cover with prepared filling.
5. Roll-up using the grease proof paper, to prevent fingers going through the pastry.
6. Place on a greased baking sheet.
7. Brush with melted butter and sprinkle with nib nuts.
8. Bake in an oven gas 4, 180°C, until golden brown.
9. Serve garnished with watercress.

Ingredients
- 150g   Mushrooms.
- 200g   Courgettes.
- 100g   Tomatoes.
- 1   Clove garlic.
- 5g   Basil.
- 50g   Mixed Nuts or Almonds.
- 50g   Butter.
- 50g   Vegetarian Cheese.
-        Sea salt and freshly ground black pepper.
- 225g   Fillo Pastry.
- 25g   Nib nuts.

Suggested Complement
Serve with salad and baked potatoes.

Processes & Recipes — Main Courses

Millet & Nut Croquettes

Yield — 5 portions

Process
1. Make a roux with the sesame oil and wholemeal flour.
2. Add the basic brown stock and cook for 12 minutes, to make a thick sauce.
3. Add millet and herbs to boiling water and simmer for 25 minutes, drain.
4. Grind the nuts in a liquidiser.
5. Sweat the onions until they are golden brown.
6. Combine all the ingredients to make a stiff dough.
7. Mould into croquette shapes, 7cm long by 3cm in diameter.
8. Pass through seasoned flour, beaten egg and breadcrumbs.
9. Deep fry at 190°C until golden brown.
10. Drain on kitchen paper and serve garnished with watercress.

Ingredients
15ml	Sesame oil.
15g	Wholemeal flour.
5ml	Mixed herbs.
200g	Millet.
900ml	Basic brown stock.
25g	Finely chopped onion.
200g	Mixed nuts.
100g	Wholemeal flour.
2	Eggs.
200g	Wholemeal breadcrumbs.
	Sea salt and black pepper.
100g	Chopped mushrooms.
2	Cloves garlic chopped.
100g	Vegetarian cheddar cheese.
10g	Chopped parsley.

Nut Loaf

Yield — 5 portions

Process
1. Line an oiled 450g bread tin with grease proof paper.
2. Sweat onions in oil or butter until they are golden brown.
3. Grind bread and nuts in a liquidizer.
4. Mix all the ingredients together.
5. Empty into the prepared tin and level the surface.
6. Bake in the oven at 200°C, gas 6, for 50 minutes or until a knife placed in the centre can be removed cleanly.

Walnut and Green Peppercorn Loaf
Process

200g	Broken walnuts.
100g	Wholemeal breadcrumbs.
20ml	Tamari.
50g	Finely chopped onions.
	Sea salt to taste.
10ml	Green peppercorns.
5ml	Chopped sage leaves.
250ml	Basic brown stock.

Note
The walnuts may be replaced by other nuts.
   The wholemeal breadcrumbs may be replaced by 50g lentils or 50g rolled oats.
   The tamari may be replaced by shoyu, vegetable or yeast extract.

Suggested Complement
Serve with braised vegetables and potatoes or green salad and a rice dish.

Processes & Recipes — Main Courses

Salads

Bulgar Wheat Salads, Green Salad, Vegetable Salad, Grain Salad, Potato Salad, Pasta Salad, Bean Salad

Bulgar Wheat Salads

Yield — 10 portions

Process
1. Soak bulgar wheat in boiling salted water or stock and leave for 1½ hours until all the liquid has been absorbed.
2. Drain and chill the cooked grain.
3. Combine grain with other ingredients.
4. Serve sprinkled with chopped parsley.

Basic Tabouli
- 400ml Bulgar wheat.
- 800ml Water or basic white stock (see Basic Preparations).
- 5g Ground Sea Salt.
- 15ml Chopped Fresh Mint Leaves.
- 5ml Chopped Chives.
- ¼ Clove crushed garlic.
- 15ml Chopped parsley.
- 40ml Olive oil.
- 20ml Lemon juice.
- 100g Chopped tomato.

Bulgar Wheat and Bean Salad
- 400ml Bulgar wheat
- 800ml Basic white stock (see Basic Preparations)
- 100g Chopped tomato
- 1 Clove garlic
- 5ml Chopped purple basil.
- 5ml Purple basil leaves.
- 100g White cooked beans — haricot, blackeye, lima beans
  Sea salt and freshly ground black pepper.

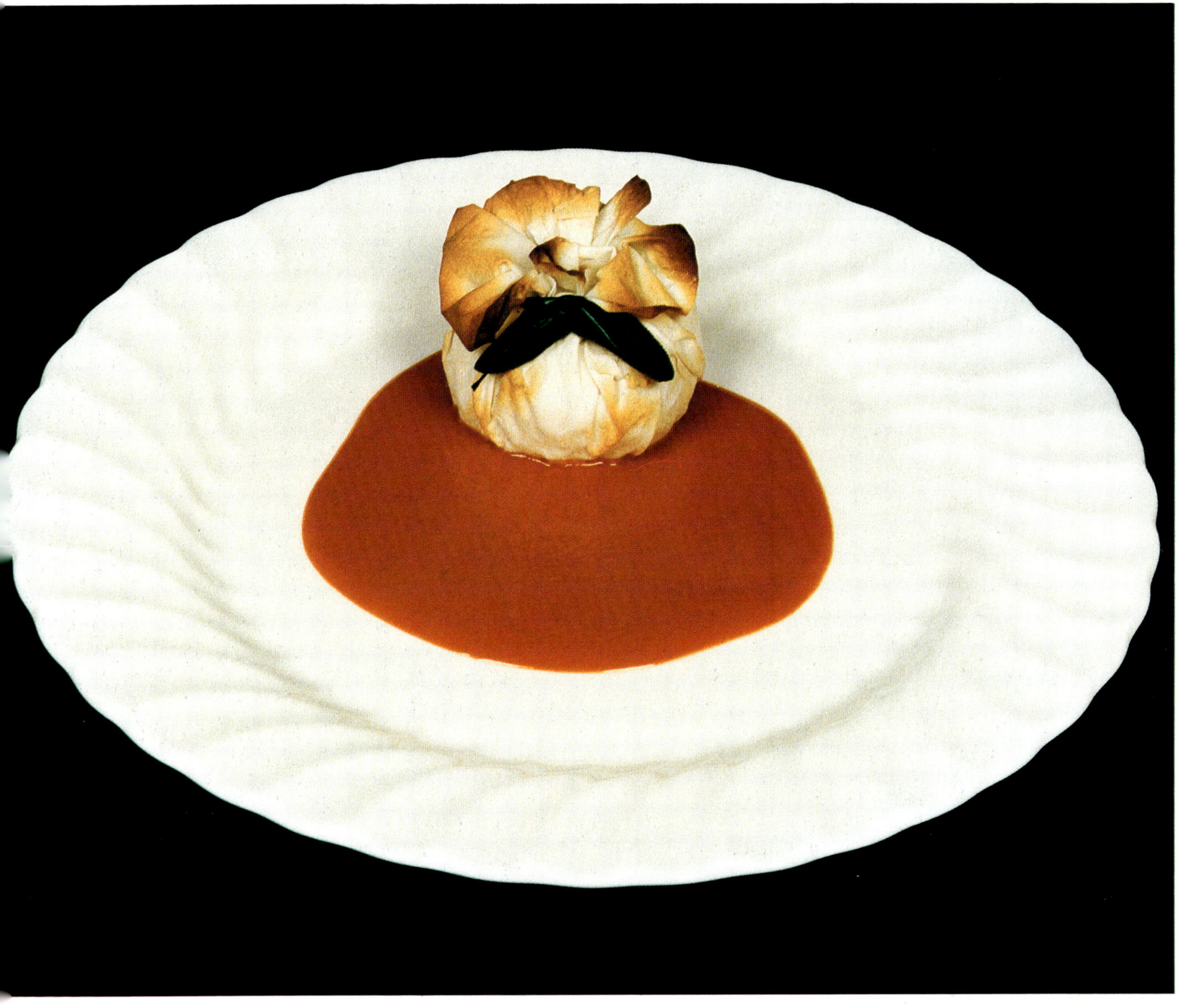

Processes & Recipes — Main Courses

Green Salad

Process
1. Pick-over and quickly wash leaf vegetables in running cold water.
2. Shake to dry.
3. Place in a large bowl and add the dressing, taking care not to drown the salad.
4. Serve in a glass bowl or on half moon side plates.

Ingredients that may be used
    Watercress.
    Fresh young spinach leaves.
    Small amounts of sorrel leaves.
    All types of lettuce.
    Chicory.
    Fennel — fern and bulb.
    Fresh mange-tout.
    Green celery.
    Green pepper.

Photograph on Page 181

To add colour and contrast use roasted nuts, radish flowers, tomato and red pepper.

Vegetable Salad

Yield — 5 portions

Process
1. Combine all blanched and raw vegetables together with the dressing.

Ingredients
50g	Baby sweetcorn, blanched.
15g	Young sorrel leaves.
25g	Mange-tout, blanched.
50g	Watercress.
25g	Stoned black olives.
10g	Pickled purple basil leaves.
50g	Blanched tomatoes de-pipped and quartered.

Processes & Recipes — Main Courses

Bean Salads

Yield 5 portions

Process
1. Soak and cook the beans separately and marinade overnight.
2. Blanch or steam the okra, refresh.
3. Drain the beans, saving the marinade.
4. Mix all the ingredients with a little of the marinade, garnish with watercress and tomato.

Ingredients
- 50g   Chick-peas.
- 50g   Black kidney beans.
- 50g   Red kidney beans.
- 50g   Flageolet beans.
- 2   Tomatoes.
- 50g   Watercress.
- 100g   Okra.

Marinade
- 50ml   White wine vinegar.
- 50ml   Sesame oil.
- 100ml   Sunflower oil.
- 2   Cloves garlic crushed and chopped.
- 15ml   Chopped tarragon.
- 15ml   Dry sherry.
- 25g   Chopped chives.
- Sea salt and freshly ground black pepper.

Dressing
- 20ml   Oil and vinegar dressing (see Basic Preparations).
- 5ml   French mustard.
- 5ml   Chopped tarragon.
- 1   Clove garlic.
- Sea salt and freshly ground black pepper.

Grain Salad

Yield — 5 portions

Process
1. Use cooked grains.
2. Marinade grains in oil and vinegar dressing.
3. Mix in nuts and seeds.
4. Fold in diced vegetables.

Ingredients
- 200g Grain — buckwheat or couscous or wheat or barley or rice.
- 30ml Oil and vinegar dressing — (see Basic Preparation).
- 25g   Mixed chopped nuts.
- 25g   Mixed seeds — sunflower — shelled pumpkin.
- Sea salt and freshly ground black pepper.

Pasta Salad

Yield — 5 portions

Process
1. Cook and refresh the pasta.
2. Mix cooked vegetables and raw vegetables.
3. With pasta and dressing.

Ingredients
- 150g Pasta — shells or macaroni or other shapes.
- 50g   Green stoned olives.
- 100g Diced tomatoes.
- 25g   Pesto dressing — (see Basic Ingredients).
- Sea salt and freshly ground black pepper.

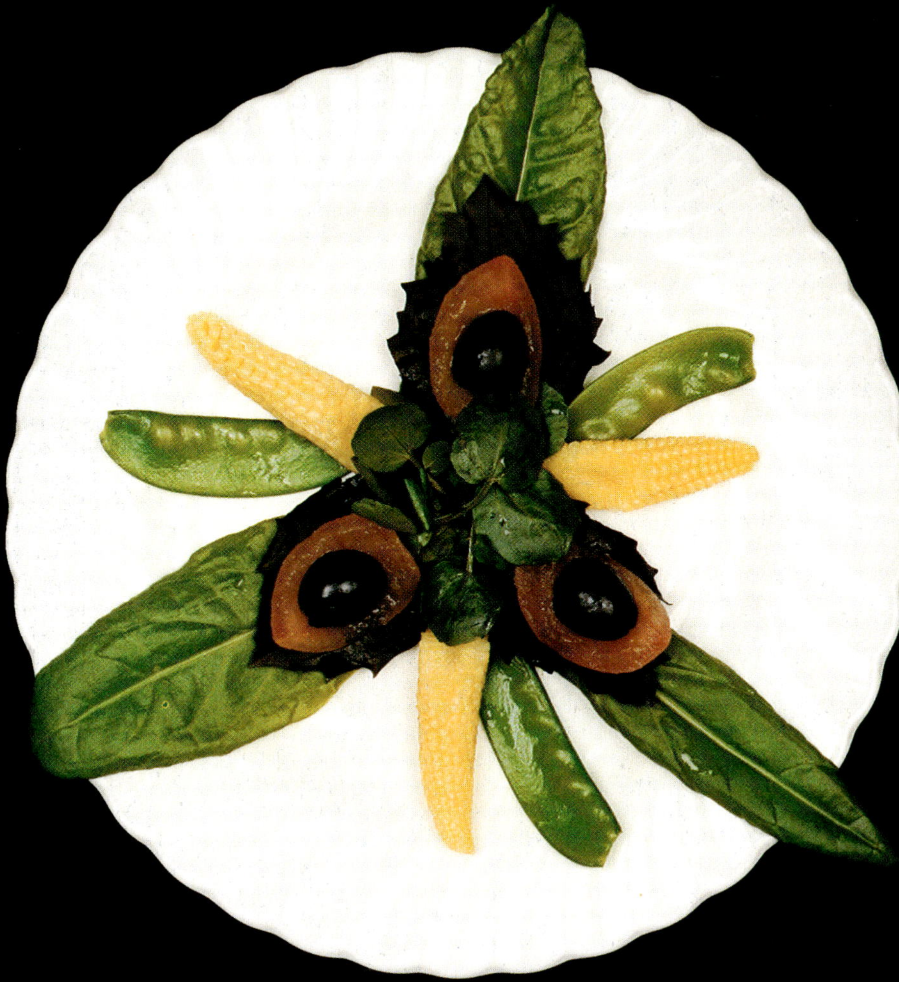

CHAPTER 7
Processes & Recipes Sweets & Savouries

Included in this chapter are a range of sweet and savoury processes which are suitable either as dessert courses on a full menu or as snack dishes in their own right. The chapter has been divided into sections as listed below. Whilst there may be fewer processes in this chapter it must be considered that the number of applications for each process is far greater because of the wide range of ingredients available for each process.

Hot Sweets
*Fruit Crumble
Baked Fruit
Fruit Pies
Steamed Fruit Pudding
Custards*

Snacks

*Egg Rolls
Mushrooms on Toast
Vegetable Pasties
Welsh Rarebit*

Cold Sweets
*Carob Mousse
Fruit Salad
Poached Fruit
Baked Pears in Fillo Pastry
Fruit Fools
Fruit Strudel
Flans
Raspberry and Peach Wendy
Sorbet
Yoghurt Cake
Icecream*

Fruit Crumble

Yield — 5 portions

Process
1. Half cook the fruit filling with honey or other sweetener.
2. Using a food processor grind and mix all the crumble ingredients.
3. Three quarter fill an oven proof dish with prepared fruit.
4. Cover with crumble mixture.
5. Bake in an oven at gas 6, 200°C, until the crumble is brown and cooked.

Crumble Mixture
- 100g   Wholemeal flour.
- 10g   Millet flakes.
- 10g   Sesame seeds.
- 100g   Chopped nuts.
- 25g   Butter.
- 20ml   Honey.

Rhubarb and Mead Crumble
- 500g   Rhubarb.
- 30ml   Mead.
- 20ml   Honey.
- 150ml   Water.
- 100g   Flour mixture crumble.

Processes & Recipes — Main Courses

Fruit Pies

Yield — 5 portions

Process
1. Wash and prepare the fruit.
2. Use a 200g flour mix of sweet wholemeal pastry.
3. Using two thirds of the pastry, line a 20cm greased flan ring.
4. Pack with the prepared fruit and other ingredients, allowing for the fruit cooking and sinking.
5. Cover with the remaining one third of pastry and notch-up the edge.
6. Brush with cold water and sprinkle with nib nuts.
7. Allow to rest for 30 minutes.
8. Bake in the oven at gas 4, 180°C, for 45 minutes.
9. Remove from flan ring and serve.

Plum Pie
- 400g   Washed and stoned plums.
- 75g   Honey.
- 100ml Water.
- 25g   Nib nuts.

Hunza Apricot Pie
- 400g   Soaked Hunza apricots (soak for 1 hour).
- 75g   Honey.
- 100ml Water.
- 20ml   Brandy.
- 25g   Ground almonds.
- 25g   Nib nuts.

Processes & Recipes — Sweets & Savouries

Baked Fruit

Yield — 5 portions

Process
1. Wash and remove the core from the fruit.
2. Score the skin of the fruit around the largest diameter in order to reduce the risk of the skin splitting.
3. Fill the space left by removal of the core with fruit mixture.
4. Stand the fruit in a roasting tray with 1cm of water in the bottom.
5. Bake in the oven at gas 4, 180°C, for 45 minutes.
6. Reduce the cooking liquid and add to a custard sauce.

Ingredients
- 5   Pears or cooking apples.

Filling
- 50g   Chopped mixed nuts.
- 50g   Chopped sultanas.
- 5g   Powdered mixed spice.
- 25g   Brown sugar or honey.

Processes & Recipes — Sweets & Savouries

Steamed Fruit Pudding

Yield — 5 portions

Process
1. Wash and prepare the fruit.
2. Use a 200g flour mix of vegetarian suet pastry.
3. Line a 1 litre (2 pint) pudding basin with two-thirds of the pastry and brush the edge with water.
4. Fill with the prepared fruit.
5. Add sugar or honey if used.
6. Roll out the remaining one-third of pastry for the lid.
7. Cover the filling and crimp the edges.
8. Cover with tin foil and steam for 1½ hours at low pressure or for 1 hour at high pressure.

Apple and Raisin
- 400g Prepared and sliced cooking apples.
- 100g Washed seedless raisins.
- 10g   Cinnamon.
- 50g   Honey.
- 45ml Water.

Custards

Yield — 5 portions

Process
1. Mix milk, beaten egg and vanilla essence.
2. Prepare moulds by coating the bottom with the topping.
3. Fill with the egg mix.
4. Place the mould in a roasting tin or an oven proof container with sides as high as the moulds.
5. Three quarters fill the roasting tin with hot water.
6. Cook in pre-heated oven at gas 5, 160°C, for 30 minutes.

Caramel Custard
- 500ml Milk.
- 4 Eggs.
- 2ml Vanilla essence.

Caramel Topping
- 100g Granulated sugar.
- 50ml Water.
- 20ml Cold water.

Process
1. Place the water and sugar in a thick bottomed pan.
2. Boil until golden in colour and small bubbles start to form at the hottest point.
3. *Off the heat and away from your face* add the cold water. This will cause a lot of steam and arrest the cooking process.,
4. Pour into prepared moulds 0.5cm deep.

Honey & Almond Custard
Custard, as for caramel custard.

Honey Topping
- 100g Liquid dark honey.
- 50g Freshly roasted nib almonds.

Processes & Recipes — Sweets & Savouries

Process
1. Warm honey to a syrup.
2. Roast almonds and add to honey.
3. Pour into prepared moulds 0.5cm deep.

Maple Syrup & Walnut Custard
    100g   Maple syrup.
    50g   Freshly roasted crushed walnuts.
Process as for honey & almond custard.

Carob Mousse

Yield — 5 portions

Process
1. Melt the carob in a small saucepan over boiling water.
2. Separate the eggs and cook the yolks with the carob until ribbon stage ie. a figure of eight can be made from the ribbon of egg from the end of the whisk.
3. Whip the double cream and fold into the mixture.
4. Whisk the egg whites to peak and fold into the mixture.
5. Pour into small pots and refrigerate to set.
6. Decorate with whipped cream.

Ingredients
    250g   Sweet Carob.
    3   Egg yolks.
    3   Egg whites.
    150ml Double cream.

Processes & Recipes — Sweets & Savouries

Fruit Salad

Yield — 5 portions

Process
1. Prepare the stock syrup by boiling the water, honey and lemon juice and allow to cool.
2. Prepare the citrus fruits such as oranges in the following way: top and tail them with a stainless steel knife, then on a board, remove peel from top to bottom using a knife to follow the curve of the fruit. Repeat until all peel is removed.
3. Remove the segments by holding the fruit in the left-hand and cutting along a segment, scrape to remove the fruit. Repeat until all segments are removed. Pips should be discarded.
4. Squeeze the pith to remove any juice.
5. Quarter and remove the core from apples and pears.
6. Remove the stones and pips from peaches, cherries and grapes.
7. Wash soft fruit and quarter, if large eg. strawberries.
8. Mix all the prepared fruit in stock syrup.
9. Peel and slice banana and add to other fruits.
10. Keep chilled.

Ingredients
2	Oranges.
1	Banana.
5	Strawberries.
2	Apple.
1	Pear.
50g	Sliced mango.
50g	Black grapes.
150ml	Water.
30ml	Honey.
15ml	Lemon juice.

Note
In place of the honey, water and lemon juice use 200ml Apple Juice.

Processes & Recipes — Sweets & Savouries

Baked Pears in Fillo Pastry

Yield — 5 portions

Process
1. Peel, core and poach the pears as for poached fruit.
2. Cool and dry the fruit.
3. Place the pear in the centre of a 12cm square of fillo pastry.
4. Fold up over the pear like a money bag.
5. Brush with butter and decorate with leaf shapes of pastry.
6. Place on a greased baking sheet and bake in the oven at gas 7, 220°C, until the pastry turns golden brown.
7. Chill and serve on a raspberry purée.

Ingredients
- 5 William pears.
- 150ml Water.
- 30ml Honey.
- 15ml Lemon juice.
- 5 Sheets of fillo pastry 20cm square.

Sauce
- 250g Frozen or fresh raspberries.
- 25g Honey.

Sauces Process
Liquidise the honey and raspberries. Seive to remove the seeds and leave to stand for 4 hours in the refrigerator.

Processes & Recipes — Sweets & Savouries

Poached Fruit

Yield — 5 portions

Process
1. If necessary, peel the fruit using a potato peeler.
2. Prepare the stock syrup by boiling ingredients together.
3. Pack the fruit into a pan deep enough to allow the stock syrup to just cover the fruit and small enough to keep the fruit upright.
4. Cover with grease proof paper.
5. Bring to the boil and simmer until just soft.
6. Cool in the stock syrup.

Stock Syrup
- 150ml   Water.
- 30ml   Honey.
- 15ml   Lemon juice.
- 2cm   Stick cinnamon.

Fruit for Poaching
Dessert Apples, Dessert Pears, Dried Apricots, Rhubarb and Prunes.

Fruit Fools

Yield — 5 portions

Process
1. Mix all ingredients together.

Ingredients
- 500g   Fruit purée.
- 300ml   Thick Greek yoghurt or whipped double cream.
- 30ml   Honey, according to taste.

Processes & Recipes — Sweets & Savouries

Fruit Strudel

Yield — 10 portions

Process
1. Peel, core and slice the fruit.
2. Prepare the breadcrumbs and liquidise.
3. Roughly chop the hazel nuts or liquidise.
4. Mix the sugar and cinnamon together.
5. Melt the butter.
6. Wash and pick over the seedless raisins.
7. Place a dry tea cloth on the table, cover with two sheets of fillo pastry with a 5cm over lap over the tea cloth.
8. Brush the pastry with melted butter.
9. Sprinkle with breadcrumbs and chopped nuts.
10. Sprinkle with sliced fruit.
11. Sprinkle with melted honey or sugar and cinnamon.
12. Roll-up using the tea towel.
13. Place on a greased tray.
14. Brush with butter.
15. Bake in the oven at 180°C, gas 4, for 35 minutes. Brush the pastry with butter as it dries out.

Ingredients
- 1.4kg Bramley apples or plums.
- 100g   Hazel nuts.
- 200g   Seedless raisins.
- 100g   Wholemeal bread.
- 100g   Brown sugar or honey.
- 2   tblsp Cinnamon.
- 75g   Salt free butter or vegetable margarine.
- 250g   Fillo pastry.

Processes & Recipes — Sweets & Savouries

Flans

Process
1. Grease a 20cm flan ring and baking sheet.
2. Roll out the pastry to a 3mm thickness.
3. Roll the pastry onto a floured rolling pin.
4. Unroll over the prepared flan ring.
5. Using a small piece of spare pastry press the pastry sheet into the flan ring taking care to remove all air spaces on the bottom and sides.
6. With the finger and thumb of the right hand make a 5mm edge around the flan.
7. Remove the spare pastry by rolling the rolling pin over the top of the flan ring.
8. Using pastry tweezers decorate the edge.
9. Bake blind by carefully lining with grease proof paper and filling with baking beans.
10. Bake in the oven at 180°C, gas 4, for 20-30 minutes.
11. Remove paper, beans and flan ring and use as required.

Gooseberry and Mango Flan

Yield — 4 portions

Process
1. Line the flan ring and bake.
2. Cook the gooseberries with the Honey and liquidise.
3. Peel and slice the mango.
4. Three quarter fill the cooled flan with gooseberry mixture.
5. Arrange slices of mango on top and coat with honey glaze or sprinkle with icing sugar and flash under a grill to brown.

Ingredients
- 150g   Sweet wholemeal pastry.
- 1   Ripe whole mango or 1 A2½ tin mango in water.
- 250g   Gooseberries.
- 15mls   Honey.
- 30mls   Honey glaze (warm honey) or 50g Icing Sugar.

Processes & Recipes — Sweets & Savouries

Raspberry and Peach Wendy

Yield — 5 portions

Process
1. Liquidise fresh raspberries with raspberry liqueur and save 5 raspberries.
2. Liquidise fresh peach with kirsch and save 5 slices.
3. Fill three piping bags fitted with a small star tube with the peach purée, raspberry purée and Greek yoghurt.
4. Pipe all three into a glass, alternating colours around the glass.
5. Top with a small slice of peach, a raspberry and mint leaf.

Ingredients
- 4 Peaches.
- 400g Raspberries.
- 10ml Raspberry Liqueur (optional).
- 10ml Kirsch (optional).
- 400ml Greek yoghurt — cows' milk.
- 5 Mint leaves.

Photograph on Opposite Page

Sorbet

Yield — 30 portions

Process
1. Freeze stock syrup, on the point of freezing.
2. Add meringue.

The flavour is changed by taking stock syrup and re-placing it with wine, fruit purée, juices etc.

Ingredients
- 1.2 Litres water) Stock syrup
- 720g Sugar) $17°C$ on a Saccharometer
- 6 Lemons (juice))
- 750ml Italienne meringue

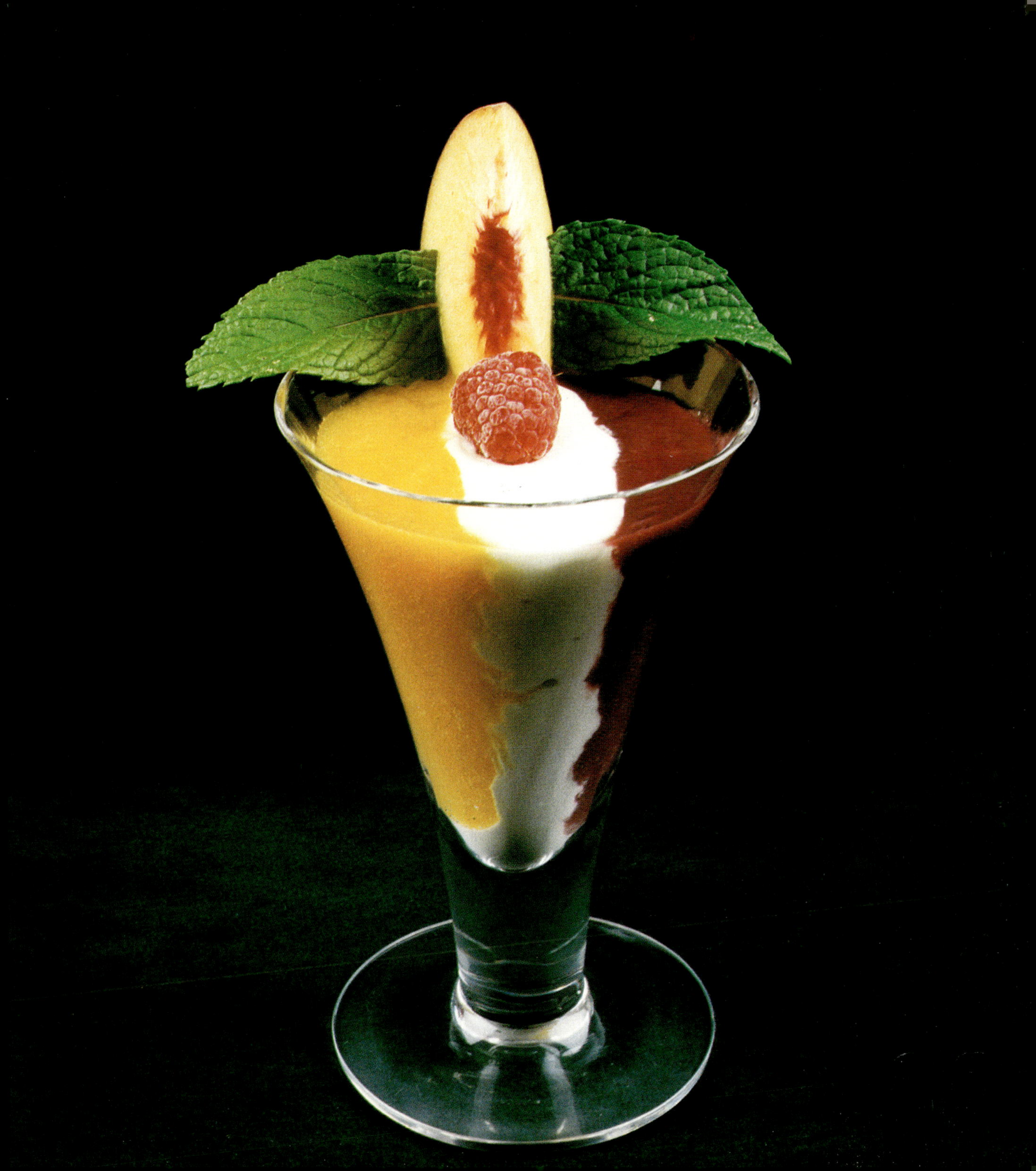

Processes & Recipes — Sweets & Savouries

Yoghurt Cake

Yield — 5 portions

Process
1. Grease and line a 20cm flan ring with sweet wholemeal pastry.
2. Bake blind (see flans) for 20 minutes.
3. Boil the water, honey and agar for 2 minutes.
4. Stir the lemon juice into the yoghurt.
5. Add the liquid agar to the yoghurt and stir to mix.
6. Boil the jam and cool.
7. Remove the flan from the oven and cool.
8. Cover the bottom of the flan case with the cool jam.
9. Fill with the setting yoghurt and cool.
10. Decorate with fresh fruit.
11. Chill before serving.
12. The fruit decoration may be glazed with honey or boiled apricot jam to prolong its life.

Ingredients
- 200g Sweet wholemeal pastry.
- 10ml Lemon juice.
- 75ml Water.
- 6g   Powdered agar.
- 480g Strained yoghurt.
- 30g   Jam.
- 100g Fresh fruit to decorate.
- 5ml   Liquid honey.

Ice-cream

Yield — 30 portions

Process
1. Cream eggs with sugar.
2. Mix with the milk and vanilla.
3. When cool add to machine.

Ingredients
- 1.2 Litres milk.
- 8 Egg yolks.
- 330g Castor sugar.
- 600ml Single cream.
- Vanilla essence.

NOTE: To every litre of milk, not less than 300 grams of sugar should be added, this will give an ice-cream that can be scooped straight from the freezer. Not more than 360 grams should be added.

1. Chocolate and coffee flavours are added to the milk before mixing with the egg yolks and sugar.
2. Whole or sliced fruits are added to the mixture at the point of freezing.
3. Purées are added after the custard is made *but* before the cream is added.

Processes & Recipes — Sweets & Savouries

Snacks

Egg Rolls, Mushrooms on Toast, Vegetable Pasties, Welsh Rarebit

Egg Rolls

Yield — 5 portions

Process
1. Heat a wok with a little corn oil.
2. Beat one egg with a little salt and pepper.
3. Fry the beaten egg in the wok to make a pancake 17cm round.
4. Remove from the wok and repeat with the other eggs.
5. Make a paste out of the flour and a little water.
6. Brush each egg round with the flour and water paste.
7. Stir fry the vegetables, fungi and spices.
8. Make a paste with the shoyu, sherry and cornflour.
9. Add the cornflour mix to the stir fried vegetables and cook for 2 minutes.
10. Fill each egg pancake with the mixture and roll-up and seal all edges.
11. Deep fry for 7-10 minutes until pancakes turn golden brown in colour.
12. Drain them on kitchen paper to remove surplus fat.

Ingredients
- 10ml   Shoyu.
- 200g   Bean sprouts.
- 150g   Mixed mushrooms — field, chanterelle, chinese.
- 15ml   Chives or Welsh onion chopped.
- 20ml   Dry sherry.
- 25ml   Cornflour.
- 5   Eggs.
- 25g   Wholemeal flour.
- 5g   Ginger root, peeled and grated.
          Sea salt and freshly ground black pepper.
- 100ml   Corn oil.
- 1   Clove garlic, peeled and finely chopped.
- 25g   Diced water chestnut.

Photograph on Opposite Page

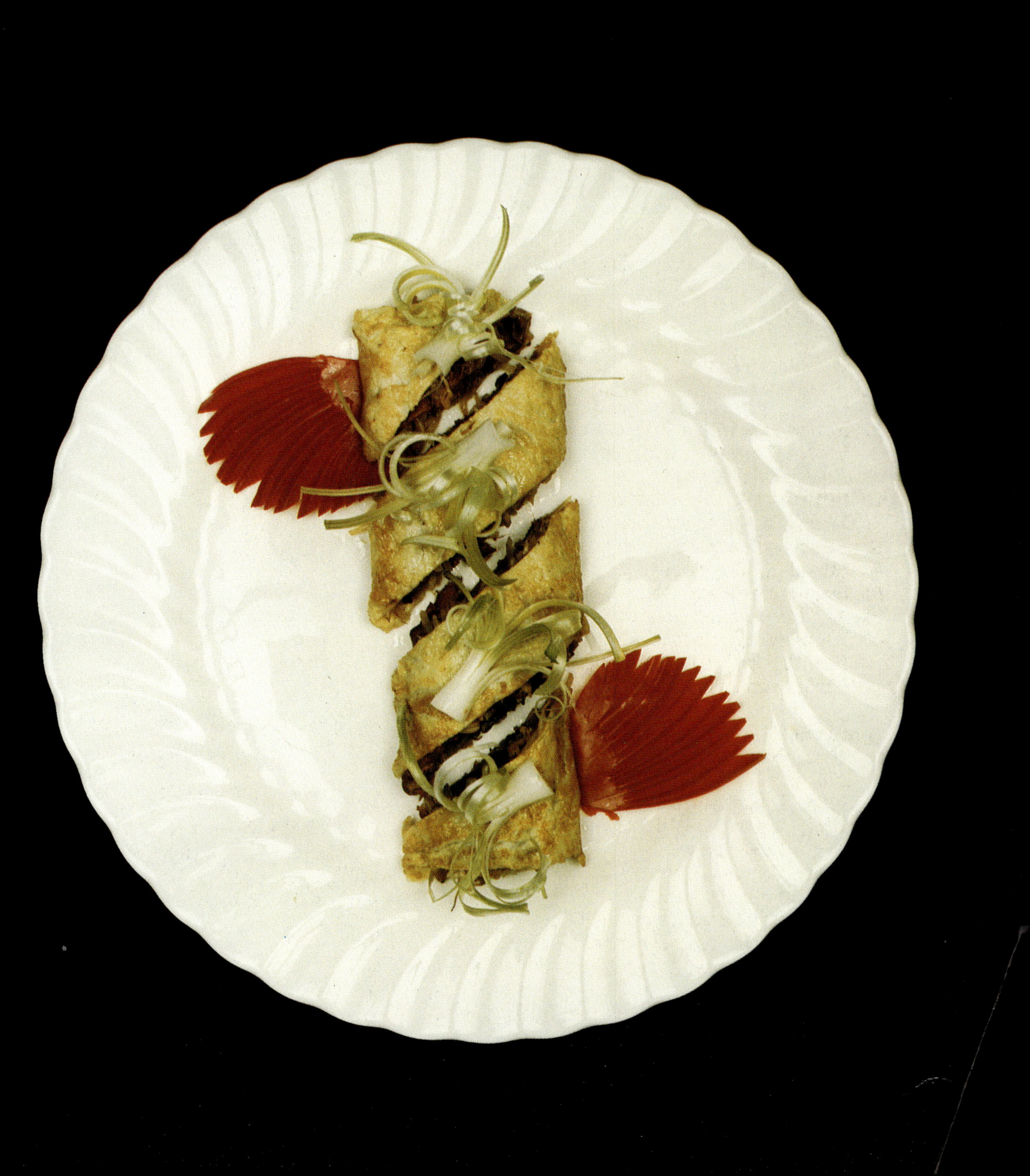

Processes & Recipes — Sweets & Savouries

Mushrooms on Toast

Yield — 5 portions

Process
1. Wash and quarter the mushrooms.
2. Heat the butter in a small saucepan and fry the curry powder.
3. Add the mushrooms and cook through.
4. Add the double cream and reboil.
5. Grill or toast the bread and spread with butter.
6. Remove any dark crusts.
7. Top with mushroom filling and garnish with chopped coriander.

Ingredients
- 5   Slices wholemeal bread.
- 250g   Button mushrooms.
- 100g   Double cream.
- 5g   Curry powder (optional).
- 15g   Butter.
-        Sea salt and freshly ground black pepper.

NOTE: Other vegetables may be used to replace mushrooms eg. courgettes, red peppers.

Vegetable Pasties

Yield — 5 portions

Process
1. Mix all the filling ingredients together and three quarters cook. Allow to cool.
2. Roll out the pastry into 20cm rounds.
3. Brush the edge with water or soya milk.
4. Divide the mixture into 5 and place a portion on each pastry round.
5. Fold over the pastry and twist the edge to seal.
6. Brush with egg or soya milk.
7. Bake in the oven for 20 minutes, at gas 6, 180°C.

Ingredients
- 300g   Savoury wholemeal pastry (see Basic Preparations).
- 100g   Cooked aduki beans.
- 100g   Cooked mushrooms.
- 100g   Diced tomatoes.
- 50g   Courgettes.
- 50g   Diced potato.
- 50g   Finely chopped and sweated onion.
- 30ml   Shoyu.
- 20ml   Chopped parsley.
- Sprig chopped sage.
- Sea salt and freshly ground black pepper.

Processes & Recipes — Sweets & Savouries

Welsh Rarebit

Yield — 5 portions

Process
1. Grill or toast the bread and spread with butter.
2. In a small saucepan reduce the brown ale by three quarters.
3. Add the white sauce, made English mustard and grated vegetarian cheddar cheese.
4. Bring to the boil.
5. Off the heat add egg yolk and season with cayenne pepper. Allow to cool.
6. Coat each slice of toast so that no toast is left uncovered.
7. Place on a tray and grill until golden brown.
8. Remove the crusts for a first class service and garnish with tomato and water cress.

Ingredients
- 150ml Basic savoury white sauce.
- 150g   Grated vegetarian cheddar.
- 80ml   Brown ale.
- 1   Egg yolk.
         Pinch cayenne.
- 2.5ml Made English mustard.
- 5   Slices wholemeal bread.
- 10g   Butter.

Buck Rarebit
Add a well drained poached egg to the finished Welsh Rarebit.

NOTE: The Savoury White Sauce may be omitted along with the egg. In which case the cheese must be increased to 400g.

Appendix 1

User Activities

1.1 List the different types of beans that are commonly available.
1.2 Briefly explain their origins and availability.
1.3 Explain their nutritional values.
1.4 Name four dishes for which these commodities are the main constituent ingredients.
1.5 Prepare a recipe for two of the dishes in 1.4
1.6 Design a recipe of your own using these commodities.
2.1 List the different types of nuts that are commonly available.
2.2 Follow activities 1.2 to 1.6 for this commodity group.
3.1 List the different methods of cookery that may be used.
3.2 List the equipment that may be used for each method.
3.3 Name a suitable dish that may be prepared by using each method.
3.4 Explain the process for two of the dishes you have chosen.
3.5 Design a recipe using alternative ingredients for the processes you have explained in 3.4.
3.6 Prepare a three course menu using a different method of cookery for each dish.
4.1 Explain the preparation and cooking of Tofu.
4.2 List four dishes using Tofu.
4.3 Explain the nutritional value of these dishes.
5.1 Explain the considerations that must be made when planning menus.
5.2 Prepare a menu for a summer cold buffet for 30 covers.
5.3 Prepare a menu for a winter cold buffet for 30 covers.
5.4 Prepare a cook to order menu for an up-market and a medium price restaurant giving a choice of 5-6 dishes for each course.
5.5 Prepare a cycle of vegetarian dishes covering 10 days for an industrial catering establishment or school serving 150 meals daily; showing a starter, one hot and one cold main course dish for each day.

Appendix

6.1 List examples of two dishes for each of the following basic preparations.
    (a) Basic brown sauce
    (b) Basic cheese sauce
    (c) Wholemeal puff pastry
    (d) Tomato sauce
    (e) Nut creams
    (f) Blini

7.1 Explain the process for purée soups.
7.2 List four purée soups from this process.
7.3 Suggest a nutritional complement for each soup.
8.1 Explain the process for baked potatoes.
8.2 Suggest five suitable fillings for baked potatoes.
9.1 Explain the process for Pizza dough and topping.
9.2 Suggest five suitable variations for toppings.
9.3 Suggest a nutritional complement for pizza.
10.1 Explain the process that may be used for any pasta dish.
10.2 List six pasta dishes from this process.
10.3 Explain the process and recipe for cottage cheese lasagne.
10.4 Suggest a nutritional complement suitable for all pasta dishes.

Appendix 2

Further Reading

TITLE	AUTHOR (PUBLISHER)
Cuisine Naturelle	Anton Mossiman (Macmillan)
Cooking With Sea Vegetables	P & M Bradford (Thorsons)
Vegetables From The Sea	S & T Arasaki (Japan Publications Inc)
The Real Food Guides 1 & 2	Cass McCallum (Molendinar Press)
Vegetarian Cookbook	Sarah Brown (Dorling-Kindersley)
Laurel's Kitchen	Robertson/Flinders/Godfrey (Routledge)
Classical Cooking The Modern Way	Eugen Pauli (CBI Publishing Co)
Raw Energy	L & S Kenton (Century)
Theory of Catering	Kinton & Ceserani (Arnold)
Purchasing, Costing & Control	Peter Odgers (G-O Publications)
Eastern Vegetarian Cookery	Madhur Jaffrey (Cape)
Cooking From An Italian Garden	Scaravelli/Cohen (Thorsons)
Greek Vegetarian Cookery	Jack Marvel (Rider)
Book Of Ingredients	Dowell/Bailey (Michael Joseph)
Composition Of Foods	McCance & Widdowsons (HMSO)
New Chinese Vegetarian Cooking	Kenneth Lo (Fontana/Collins)
Vegetarian Bar-be-cue	David Eno (Thorsons)
Crank's Recipe Book	J.M. Dent & Sons Ltd
Herb & Spice Booklets	Herb Society

Index

Additive free	1	Bread quick	156	Coriander herb	32
Aduki beans	10	Broad beans	10	Coriander seed	48
Aduki bean & mushroom		Broccoli cheese	144	Cranks	6
pudding	150	Brotherton, Joseph	1	Cream	17
Aerosol cream	18	Brown rice	26	Cumin	49
Agar	40	Brazil nut	36	Currants	19
Almonds sweet	40	Btec	6		
Allspice	45	Buck rarebit	202	Dairy products	14
Anna style potatoes	148	Buckwheat	24	Dates	20
Anise	45	Buckwheat flour	28	Dauphine potatoes	149
Anise star	45	Bulgar wheat	27	Davies, Richard	1, 6
Apricot	19	Bulgar wheat salads	176	Definitions	8
Arame	40	Bulgar wheat & bean salad	176	Fruit diet	8
Asafoetida	46	Butter	16	Lacto-vegetarian	8
Ashen, David	6	Butter beans	10	Macrobiotic	8
Avocado cocktail	116	Butter lactic	16	Vegan	8
		Butter milk	16	Dietary fibre	108
Baking	85	Butter sweet	16	Diet balanced	108
Baked potatoes	147	Button mushrooms	22	Dill herb	32
Baked fruit	185	Canellini bean	11	Dill seed	49
Baked pears in fillo pastry	190	Carob mousse	188	Double cream	17
Baked sliced potatoes	146	Caramel custard	187	Dressings	70
Bakers style potatoes	147	Caraway	46	Cashewnut & gooseberry	74
Balanced diets	108	Carbohydrate	101	Oil & vinegar	70
Bananas	19	Cardamoms	46	Pesto	75
Barley	24	Carrageen	41	Yoghurt	70
Barley flour	28	Cashew	37	Dried milks	15
Barley malt	24	Cauliflower cheese	144	Filled milk	15
Barley pearl	24	Cayenne	47	Skimmed	15
Basic preparations	53	Celery seed	47	Whole	15
Basil purple	31	Cep	21	Duchesse potato	149
Basil sweet	30	Channel Island milk	14	Dulse	41
Basmati rice	26	Chanterelle	22	Dumplings pasta	161
Batters	76	Cheese	16		
Batter pancake	76	Chervil	31	Evaporated milk	16
Bay sweet	31	Chestnut sweet	37	Fats	102
Bean bags	169	Chick peas	10	Fennel garden	32
Bean curry	171	Chickpea pate-hummus	115	Fennel florence	32
Bean goulash	170	Chickpea & pepper couscous	152	Fennel seed	49
Bean salads	179	Chinese black bean	10	Field bean	10
Bean soup	127	Chinese mushrooms	22	Figs	20
Bean stew	170	Chilli	47	Fillo cake savoury	154
Bean & vegetable pancakes	169	Chipp, Beverley	6	Flageolet beans	12
Blackeye beans	10	Chives	32	Flans	193
Blanching	83	Cinnamon	48	Gooseberry & mango	193
Blini	77	City & Guilds	6	Flat mushrooms	23
Blini with leeks & mushrooms	164	Clotted cream	17	Fleiss, Walton	5
Boiling	86	Cloves	48	Folic acid	105
Booth, Bramwell	1	Coconut	37	Fruit cocktail	114
Borage	31	Cocktail sauce	74	Fruit crumble	183
Braising	82	Commodity purchase sizes	109	Fruit diet	8
Braised brown rice	167	Condensed milk	15	Fruit fool	191
Braised millet	167	Converted rice	24	Fruit pies	184
Bread naan	159	Couscous	27	Fruit salad	189
Bread pitta	158	Cooking methods	81	Fruit strudel	192

206

Index

Frying deep	83	Methods of preparations & cutting	88
Frying shallow	84	Mayonnaise	71
Gallup polls	2	Mayonnaise vegan	72
Garlic	33	Microwave	86
Gaufrette potatoes	148	Millet braised	167
Gazpacho	120	Millet common	25
Ginger	49	Millet & nut croquettes	174
Grains cooking	54	Milks	14-16
Grain salad	180	Mint apple	34
Green salad	178	Miso	43
Greek yoghurt	18	Miso soup	123
Grilling	85	Mineral elements	107
		Mung beans	13
Half cream	17	Mushroom & pasta cocktail	116
Haricot beans	12	Mushrooms on toast	200
Hardboiled eggs	137	Mustard (three types)	50
Haywards Hotel	1		
Hazelnuts	37	Naan bread	159
Hijiki	18	Noodles with sauce	163
Homogenised milk	14	Nori	42
Honey & almond custard	187	Nut creams	73
Horn of plenty	22	Nutrition	101
Hotelympia	5	Nutmeg	50
Hot stuffed mushrooms	117		
Hunza apricot pie		Oats	25
Hyssop	33	Ohsawa, George	8
		Okara	43
Ice-cream	197	Omelets	138
		Omelet vegetable	139
Kidney beans	12	Oregano	33
Kidney bean soup	125	Ovid	1
Kombu	42		
		Pancake batter	76
Lactic butter	16	Pancakes bean & vegetable	169
Lacto-vegetarian	8	Paper bag cooking	87
Lasagne	165	Paprika	51
Laver	41	Parsley	34
Leeks in cheese sauce	144	Parsley flat	35
Lee, Maxwell	2	Pasta dumplings	161
Lentils	13	Pasta salad	14
Lentil & nut cake	172	Pasteurised milk	57
Lentil soup	124	Pasties vegetable	201
Lima beans	12	Pasties deep fried	201
Low fat	1	Pate	115
		Chickpea (hummus)	115
Macadamia nut	38	Mushroom & nut	116
Mace	50	Mushroom & lentil	115
Macrobiotic	8	Peanut	38
Maize	25	Pearl barley	24
Maple syrup & walnut custard	188	Peas	13
Marjoram pot	33	Pecan	38
Marquis potatoes	149	Penguin	5
Marsh samphire	42	Pepper	51
Maxwell, Lee	2	Pesto	75
Menu planning	92	Pine nuts	38
Menu planning considerations	93	Pistachio	39
Menu examples	94-100	Pitta bread	158

Pizza	155
Plato	1
Plum pie	184
Plymouth College of F.Ed	6
Poaching	82
Poached eggs	136
Poached egg with mushoom & sweetcorn	
Poached egg with spinach & cheese	
Poached fruit	191
Potato dishes	146
Pot roast vegetables	145
Pot roast courgettes	146
Pot roast green pepper & carrot	146
Pot roast red pepper & parsnips	146
Proteins	102
Prunes	20
Puffball giant	23
Pulses cooking of	55, 56
Pumpkin seed	39
Pythagoras	1
Raised pie	151
Raisins	21
Raspberry & peach Wendy	194
Ratatouille	141
Reading University	2
Realeat Company	2, 3, 4, 5
Rhubarb & mead crumble	183
Rice cakes with spinach & sweetcorn	166
Rice	25
Rice flour	29
Roasting	87
Rolled curried pancakes	169
Rolled oats	25
Roulade — spinach	130
Rosemary	35
Rye	27
Saffron	57
Sage common	35
Salvation Army	1
Sauces	64
Brown	64
Cheese	69
Cocktail tahini	74
Mayonnaise	71
Vegan mayonnaise	72
Red pepper	68
Spinach	67
Sweet & sour mushroom	69
Tomato	67
White	64
Sweet white	64
White stock	64
White vegetable	65
Warm	66

207

Index

Savoury flans	139	Sweating	83
Savoury winter	35	Swiss style potatoes	147
Scrambled eggs	134	Sweets hot & cold	182
with courgettes & olives	135		
with mushrooms	135	Tamari	43
Semi skimmed milk	14	Tarragon french	36
Semolina	28	Tempeh	44
Sesame seeds	39	Tempura	117
Set type yoghurt	18	Thyme garden	36
Shaw, George Bernard	1	Tofu	44, 56
Shoyu	44	Tolstoi, Count	1
Single cream	17	Tomato mousse	119
Skimmed milk	15	Tomato soup fresh	126
Snacks	202	Truffle	23
Sorbet	194	Turmeric	52
Sorrel	36	Turning mushrooms	90
Souffle	131	Turning vegetables	89
Cheese	131	T.V.P. (Textured Vegetable	
Broccoli	134	Protein)	44
Leek	134		
Spinach	134	Ultra heat treated (UHT) cream	18
Soups	119	UHT milk	15
Soured cream	17	Useful information	78, 79
Soya	13		
Spaghetti with sauce	162	Vanilla	52
Spearmint	34	Vegan	8
Spices	45	Vegan Society	2
Spoon moulding	91	Vega Restaurant	5
Steaming	84	Vegetable cocktail	116
Steaming without pressure	85	Vegetable dips	117
Steaming under pressure	85	Vegetable mousse	119
Steamed fruit puddings	186	Vegetable pasties	201
Stewing	81	Vegetable preparation	88
Stewed okra & tomatoes	141	Vegetable & pesto soup	128
Stewed peas	141	Vegetable salad	178
Stewed vegetables	140	Vegetarian Association	6
Sterilised cream	17	Vegetarian Children's society	2
Sterilised half cream	17	Vegetarian Messenger	1
Sterilised milk	15	Vegetarian Nutritional	
Stir fried vegetables	145	Research Centre	2
Stir fried vegetables in		Vegetarianism	8
a basket	145	Vegetarian Society	1, 2
Stir type yoghurt	18	Vegetarian, The	2
Stock	62	Vitamins	103-106
Brown	62		
Concentrate	63	Wakame	42
White	62	Walnut	39
Stroganoff courgette	142	Walnut & green peppercorn	
Stroganoff mushroom	142	loaf	175
Stuffed peppers	143	Water	108
Stuffed peppers with		Welsh rarebit	202
mushrooms & almonds	143	Wheat	27, 30
Student questions	203	Whipping cream	17
Suet pudding	150, 186	White bean soup	125
Sultanas	21	Wild rice	26
Sunflower seeds	40	Wok	84
Sweet almonds	40		
Sweet chestnut	37	Yang	8
		Yin	8
		Yoghurt	18